"Whether you are a company of three or 30,000 employees, *Road to Respect* is a must read... Erica's depth of experience is clearly evident throughout the entire book. It has given me practical tools in representing my membership..."

—PAUL ALTILIA, business agent member and labour relations, Manager of Directors Guild of Canada, British Columbia

"With her trademark straightforward style, Erica presents engaging stories, powerful insights and concrete strategies for achieving respectful workplaces. Erica's highly readable book is unique in its attention to the Canadian context. A terrific resource for leaders who want to make a positive difference in their organizations!"

—DR. RHONDA L. MARGOLIS, principal, RLM Learning Innovations

"This book will help you identify and effectively manage the 'elephant' in your workplace. I urgently recommend you read *Road to Respect* and benefit from Erica's commitment and dedication to improving the work environment."

—LARRY JOHNS, general manager, screening operations, BC and Ft. McMurray, GARDA

"Erica Pinsky has hit on what is, for both employees and employers, the key to sustained business success: an organizational culture embodying behaviours that lead to a work environment "where employees feel safe, included and respected" – where they are encouraged and supported to "take responsibility, resolve their conflicts and take action when they witness disrespectful behaviour." This is a topic all of us need to know more about. Given Erica's consulting professionalism focused on respect in the workplace, her book should be a great source of information and inspiration."

—RON EINBLAU, president, Einblau & Associates

"There is simply no downside to having the kind of workplace environment that attracts good people. In a competitive environment you are not just competing for customers, but for staff too. Service to customers and clients, the lifeblood of my business, depends on a team that feels valued and supported. Erica Pinsky understands how employers can be Employers of Choice."

—BARRY CAMPBELL, president, Campbell Strategies

"Respect in the workplace is key for any business wanting to attract and retain an engaged workforce in a diverse marketplace. Erica's book, *Road to Respect*, offers a comprehensive roadmap to profitability for organizations looking to conquer many of today's toughest business challenges and be recognized as Employers of Choice."

—HUNTER ROGERS, vice president, labour relations & safety, Coast Mountain Bus Company

"Storytelling is an incredibly powerful means of teaching. In *Road to Respect* Erica once again uses stories to inform and engage readers. Her book offers compelling perspectives as to why building a respectful workplace culture truly is the Path to Profit in today's highly diverse and complex business environment."

—MARNI JOHNSON, CHRP, vice president, human resources and communications, North Shore Credit Union

"Businesses are built on relationships, and lasting relationships require ongoing, mutual respect. Erica Pinsky's book, *Road to Respect: Path to Profit,* offers readers valuable insights and practical strategies for creating adaptable workplaces characterized by communication, trust and respectful relationships. This book is a must read for anyone seeking success in today's complex business environment."

—DAVID W. HAMILTON, president, Focus Entertainment Insurance Brokers Inc

"Society is changing and workplaces have to adjust to the expectations of both employees and the broader society within which we work. Our organization placed the establishment of a respectful workplace as a high priority and Erica Pinsky assisted us greatly in moving toward the achievement of that objective. Her extensive knowledge and experience make *Road to Respect* required reading for anyone interested in respect at work."

—KEN NOVAKOWSKI, executive director, British Columbia Teachers' Federation

"When Erica speaks on respectful workplaces, you can see the passion in her presence and hear it in her presentation. It also infuses every page of this very fine book she has now written. It is passion tempered with the wisdom that comes from experience and reflection. It is passion communicated with wit and clarity. It is passion that will inspire you to become an employer of choice in an increasingly tough labour market for the brightest and best. It is passion that will benefit your bottom lines – profit, productivity and social wellbeing."

—BRIAN J. FRASER, PHD, lead provocateur, Jazzthink

"My business has a truly global customer base. Success in a global environment requires business relationships built on a foundation of respect and trust. In her book, *Road to Respect: Path to Profit*, Erica Pinsky shows readers how to create those win/win relationships. While its Canadian perspective will make it particularly relevant to Canadian employers, any organization interested in creating a workplace that attracts and retains the best and brightest in today's multicultural talent pool will benefit from applying the practices Erica shares in this engaging and stimulating book."

—JERRY A. ROSENBLATT, PHD., Centre of Excellence leader, global forecasting & opportunity assessment, IMS Consulting

"Employees are placing an ever-increasing importance on corporate culture – they want a comfortable work environment where they can reach their potential. Organizations that create and maintain such an environment will have superior employee performance and gain a recruiting and retention advantage. Erica is a passionate and skilled advocate for the type of respectful workplace all forward-looking corporations are trying to achieve. *Road to Respect* will show employers how to get there."

—DAVID HUMER, manager, Commercial Credit, TD Canada Trust

"Erica Pinsky is on the right path... The Golden Rule is so very important. Mary Kay Ash based her company Mary Kay Cosmetics on the Golden Rule forty-five years ago and today it is still going strong with over 1.7 million Beauty Consultants in over thirty markets worldwide."

—PHYLLIS KEENIE, sales director, Mary Kay Cosmetics

"Employers who wish to create 'happy cultures' need to buy *Road to Respect: Path to Profit* by Erica Pinsky. In our ever changing face of business with different cultures, generations and other challenges, Erica's book is a roadmap that will help businesses prosper and individuals thrive."

—CHERYL CRAN, CSP (Certified Speaking Professional), author of *The Control Freak Revolution, 50 Ways to Lead & Love It* and *Say What You Mean - Mean What You Say*

"Having known and worked with Erica Pinsky for many years, I was delighted to hear that she intended to put her practical lessons in building a respectful workplace culture into a book. And the book is everything one might hope it to be. A frank assessment of power, fear and disrespectful behaviours in the workplace, and the solutions needed to turn it around. A must for employers needing to avoid human rights liability, but also for creating a wonderful place to work for everybody."

—SUSAN O'DONNELL, executive director, BC Human Rights Coalition

"With the first of the baby boomers beginning to retire, businesses are making retaining and recruiting new talent a high priority. Those that are ready to embrace this challenge will find Erica's book, *Road to Respect*, invaluable, as it lays the foundation of how to create a positive and efficient work environment that employees will not want to leave. The best part is, it does not require a lot of financial capital: only the will to embrace the fundamental principles shared in this book."

—KAMAL BASRA, investment advisor, TD Waterhouse Private Investment Advice

"A belief I have lived by throughout my career is the requirement to lead by example. In *Road to Respect*, Erica Pinsky presents compelling arguments as to why leaders and those they lead should chose to walk the talk of respect at work. This book will prove invaluable for anyone interested in building a truly cohesive, responsive and profitable organization in today's challenging business environment."

—SUE PAISH, CEO, Pharmasave Drugs (National) Ltd..

"Erica Pinsky's book, *Road to Respect: Path to Profit*, approaches a range of difficult topics in an honest, direct and non-threatening manner. This book will stimulate readers to think about their own values and behaviours and to question those that are operating in their workplaces. Erica shares personal stories and best practices to clearly show why adopting respect as a core value is a requirement for any business interested in being designated as an Employer of Choice in our multicultural workplaces. I highly recommend this book!"

—SUSAN RUBIN MULDER, principal, McKinsey & Company

"*Road to Respect* tackles many of the toughest issues we face in business today. Erica's insight provides practical information and sound guidance for our leadership team in our journey to be recognized as an Employer of Choice."

—DAVE HOOD, CEO, The Original Cakerie Ltd.

"At Pacific Blue Cross we have seen how Erica's respectful strategies work to create a healthier and more productive workplace. In *Road to Respect*, Erica provides employers with important, practical information to get them on the Path to Profit."

—ANNE KINVIG, senior vice president, human resources, Pacific Blue Cross

"In *Road to Respect*, Erica Pinsky writes 'A respectful union management relationship does not mean a relationship without disagreement ᴏ conflict. But as long as there is dialogue and an interest in resolving an issue, the process and relationship reflect respect.' This book is a great resource for those in the unionized workplace interested in a true win/win outcome for business, the union and the employees."

—KEN SAUNDERS, vice chair, BC Labour Relations Board.

ROAD TO RESPECT: PATH TO PROFIT

How to Become an

EMPLOYER OF CHOICE

by Building a

RESPECTFUL

WORKPLACE CULTURE

ERICA PINSKY

Library and Archives Canada Cataloguing in Publication

Pinsky, Erica Jill
Road to respect: path to profit : how to become an employer of choice by building a respectful workplace culture.

Includes bibliographical references.

ISBN 978-0-9811461-0-2

1. Respect for persons. 2. Work environment. 3. Corporate culture. I. Title.

HD58.7.P55 2009   658.3'145   C2008-907963-9

Editing by Pam Withers
Proofreading by Melissa Edwards
Book Design by Fiona Raven
Author Photo by Sandra Steier

First Printing 2009
Printed in Canada

Erica J. Pinsky Inc.
www.ericajpinskyinc.ca

Mixed Sources
Cert no. SW-COC-001271
© 1996 FSC
FSC

To my late husband, David Joachim Haiduga,
whose undying love and unwavering support
continues to sustain me,

and

to my daughter Abee,
who helped me rediscover the power of hope,
and inspires me to walk the talk of respect.

Contents

Introduction

I am not young enough to know everything.

—OSCAR WILDE

ONE DECEMBER EVENING I was sitting in my car with my three-year-old daughter Abee, waiting to get out of a McDonald's drive-through. I had picked her up from daycare, I had Christmas shopping to do, she was hungry and my husband was working late.

So as soon as I'd picked up our food, I headed up the exit lane. At the end of that lane was a large and prominent "right turn only" sign. And of course, right in front of me was a van with its left turn signal flashing.

"Okay," I thought, "no big deal; it will take only a minute." I myself have been known to disobey the occasional traffic indicator. As Abee chattered away, I focused on the steady stream of traffic preventing the woman ahead of me from making her illegal left turn.

A minute turned into two, then three. I honked repeatedly, but to no avail. I was getting madder by the minute.

"Read the sign," I muttered. "What is the matter with you? Come on, lady, I have a life here!" I honked and finally shouted, "Oh, for crying out loud, you stupid woman, read the sign! Just turn right and let me out of here!"

A little voice from the back asked, "What's the matter, Mommy?"

"The stupid woman ahead is trying to turn left when it says she can only turn right, honey. That's why we're stuck."

"Mommy, it's not nice to call someone stupid. It hurts their feelings."

Okay, I'm in the business of promoting respectful relationships in the workplace and I certainly wanted to model respectful behaviour to my small daughter. So I said, "Well, you are right, sweetie, but it doesn't matter. She can't hear me." I honked again.

"Mommy," Abee pressed, "I heard you call that lady stupid. It would hurt my feelings if you called me stupid. Maybe she heard you, too, and you hurt her feelings. You need to apologize to her."

"Oh, for Pete's sake!" I muttered. "What next?" Trying to project calm, I said, "Abee, you're right. I shouldn't have called her stupid, but I'm sure she didn't hear me and she won't hear me if I apologize now."

"No, Mommy. You have to say you're sorry."

At that moment, a break in traffic allowed the van to pull out. "Hurry, Mommy, hurry!" Abee piped up. "Apologize right now before it's too late!"

What could I do? "Okay, sweetie." Feeling like a complete idiot, I rolled down my window and shouted, "Lady in the van: I am very sorry I called you stupid."

As we finally pulled out, Abee said, "That was good, Mommy. I feel much better now that you said you were sorry."

For Abee, the matter was crystal clear. You don't call people names because it hurts their feelings. And if you do call them names, you have to apologize. There was no way out – no way to rationalize, justify or defend my bad and hurtful behaviour.

Fast forward a few years: I was driving Abee (now eight years old) and her friend to gymnastics. They were in the back seat discussing a girl in their class in a gossipy manner. And hey, I am in the business of promoting respectful behaviour.

"Sorry for interrupting you, girls, but what I'm hearing from you sounds like gossip, which as you know can be a kind of bullying."

The back seat occupants went silent. Then came, "It's not really gossip... She's not here... She won't know..."

"Sorry, girls, none of that makes any difference to me. I'm uncomfortable listening to gossip about your friend and I don't want to want to hear it anymore."

Another moment of silence, then Abee said, "Okay, you're right, Mom. We won't talk about her anymore."

As I dropped them off, I wondered what had happened to the three-year-old girl who had been so clear about the wrong in saying hurtful things. Then I reminded myself of all the influences she'd encountered since age three, and how my job was merely to do what I could to raise an assertive, empathic and respectful child. To that end, I needed to correct her, as I'd just done, as well as model the proper behaviour, as I'd done at her urging five years earlier. All so that Abee and her friend would know what behaviour was expected of them in my car.

I have been consulting for over ten years. Clients call me when there is a problem. Sometimes someone has filed a complaint; sometimes the complaint has been dealt with and the court settlement demanded that they bring in training. In some cases, companies call me to resolve issues that have been festering for many years.

I do what I can, but too often it feels like I'm placing a Band-Aid on a gangrenous wound. I have worked with employers on issues ranging from discrimination and bullying to interpersonal conflict. I write Respectful Workplace policies and provide training. I am very good at what I do, but I can achieve long-lasting success only when I can persuade the firm to examine and re-structure its core culture.

Problem workplace behaviour does not occur in a vacuum. Like bacteria, it needs the right conditions to grow. It grows best in an unhealthy organizational culture.

The world around us has changed dramatically in the last fifty years. So has the workplace. The way we work, the type of people we work with and the laws that apply to the workplace are in a constant state of flux. Change is happening so quickly that it is hard to keep up. But one thing has not changed: the employer still holds ultimate power in the workplace.

This fact is recognized in law, and to a large extent, that is why I have such a busy consulting practice. If employers actually used their power to comply with the intention of the law, I would be far less busy.

Canadian laws demand that employers create a Respectful Workplace, one free from discrimination and harassment. In Quebec, the law has gone even further to legislate a workplace free from psychological harassment, or what I refer to as workplace bullying.

Most of the time, employers respond to these laws reactively rather than proactively. They aren't concerned with compliance at all until someone raises a complaint, at which point they typically shrug it off as an isolated incident – rather than as the tip of an iceberg. The iceberg, bobbing unseen beneath the surface, is the workplace culture from which the complaint sprang.

Until recently, this reactive posture may have been enough. When there are more people than jobs, the employer is particularly powerful. Employees stay despite an unhealthy work environment. However, when there are more jobs than people, the power balance shifts. Employees no longer remain in a job that makes them feel excluded or disrespected.

Just last week, a former participant in one of my Respectful Workplace Training classes phoned to tell me he was feeling discouraged and disillusioned. His manager's disrespectful behaviour had not abated as the result of my course. "Confidentially," he said, "there are so many jobs out there that we are all looking around."

We are living in a multicultural, socio-political environment that is well informed about human rights. In fact, we are witnessing a generation of workers both community minded and action oriented.

It is only logical that, given a choice, people will choose to work where they feel comfortable, appreciated and included. Most people will not choose a work environment where they feel disrespected or excluded, or witness ongoing conflicts and abusive behaviour. Study after study has shown that money is not the main factor keeping employees in a job. People stay because of workplace culture and relationships.

When employees need their jobs, they put up with a toxic culture because they have to. However, as Bob Dylan wrote so many years ago, "The times they are a-changing." Organizations that want to survive and prosper in the new millennium need to recognize the dramatic effect their workplace culture has on their bottom line. Employers who want to be profitable in business have to make deliberate and strategic choices about their workplace culture.

As a consultant, I can write a Respectful Workplace policy – which often includes a very specific code of conduct. I can provide the training and tell people what they have to do to create a respect-ful workplace. However, I have absolutely no power to make that happen. Culture change results only when the employer (who, as we have already established, is legally in a position of power in the workplace) makes a decision to embark on a deliberate strategy to create a respectful workplace, and reinforces that strategy with a lead-by-example philosophy.

That day with Abee and her friend in the car, I realized I had to make a choice and take action. I was clear about my parenting goals and I had the power to make the rules. Had I not said anything at the time, it would become increasingly challenging to correct that behaviour. I had to be clear about what I expected and encourage open dialogue about the issue. I also had to ensure that I modelled the behaviour I expected to see from my daughter.

Modelling is the biggest challenge. I know I have been success-ful in raising an assertive, confident child every time my daughter accurately and respectfully points out my behavioural shortcomings.

Her feedback works because I value my relationship with her and don't want to lose her respect.

We have all heard that most employees spend more time at work than they do with their own families. People today come to the workplace with a host of differences in experience, outlook, temperament and behaviour. In a multicultural country like Canada, these differences can be sharply pronounced. Can any employer in the reality of today's marketplace afford to assume that everyone will work together productively?

In the workplace, I see the solution but lack the power to implement it. It's employers who decide what behaviours will contribute to a productive and thriving workplace, and manage accordingly. Employers have the power to create a profitable culture where employees feel safe, included and respected. Employers have the power to create a culture that empowers employees to take responsibility, resolve their conflicts and take action when they witness disrespectful behaviour.

It isn't enough to resolve one complaint, adopt a policy or provide training. It may be enough for minimum legal compliance, but it is not a win/win solution. The workplaces that achieve the latter commit to a respectful culture just as they tackle workplace safety.

Those are the clients who inspire and motivate me. Those are the workplaces where complaints of discrimination, harassment and bullying rarely occur because they are now at odds with the corporate culture. Conflicts are acknowledged and dealt with respectfully. These workplaces are cohesive, adaptive and inclusive. They celebrate the diversity of their employees and encourage ongoing discourse and dialogue about these differences. Individual employees feel valued, empowered and connected to the corporation. Employees love to work in such workplaces, and employers make the profits they desire.

I wrote this book to share my vision of respectful workplaces and provide proof that it is realistic and achievable. To this end, I have included the stories of some of the most successful businesses in Canada, businesses that are recognized as Employers of Choice by their employees and the business community. These Employers of Choice understand the correlation between their respectful workplace culture and their business success.

My goal, in effect, is to put myself out of a job. Let's face it – if my vision is realized, why would anyone need to hire me?

I am passionate about promoting my vision. I hope, as you read this book, some of that passion rubs off on you. As the late Christopher Reeve said, "So many of our dreams at first seem impossible, then they seem improbable and then, when we summon the will, they soon become inevitable."

What is your vision for your workplace? Summon your will and read on...

Part 1

Power, Respect and
Workplace Culture

1

Choosing to Walk the Talk

When all is said and done, a lot more is said than done.

—LOU HOLTZ, Notre Dame football team coach

IN 1959, YOUNG architect Isadore "Issy" Sharp was designing buildings and houses for his father's Toronto construction firm when he got involved in a downtown motel design project. That's when Sharp realized what he really wanted to do. He wanted to design and run his own hotels.

Sharp was a doer, not a talker. He quit his job, raised some money and in 1960 founded the Four Seasons Hotels Corporation. A year later he opened his first hotel in downtown Toronto.

Sharp had a clear vision. He knew that he wanted to cater to the luxury traveller. And he knew he wanted to succeed. From the start, Sharp knew that his most valuable asset would be his employees. He began building a corporate culture that ensured every employee working for him felt valued and respected. Sharp believed that if his staff felt appreciated and esteemed, they would deliver exceptional service and make hotel guests feel valued and respected.

He decided to make the "Golden Rule" the cornerstone of the Four Seasons' corporate culture: "Treat others as you would like to be treated."

Sharp's decision predated the legal obligation to promote respect and dignity in the workplace by twenty-five years. He based his corporate culture on the Golden Rule for one reason. He knew it made good business sense.

Some of his senior people scoffed at the idea of the Golden Rule culture, and this worried him. "If we were seen only as caring about profits and prestige rather than about our customers and our employees, there would be no belief in our values, and we would be communicating across a trust gap. We aimed to treat others as we would want to be treated ourselves. Enforcing our credo was the hardest part, and senior managers who couldn't or wouldn't live by it were weeded out within a few years. That was painful, but it had to be done."[1]

A key component to Sharp's corporate culture plan was his financial strategy. He needed the money to support his vision of a Golden Rule culture. So, rather than tie up his capital in real estate, he partnered with hotel owners, thereby leaving enough financial resources to invest in his employees. He focused on recruitment, training and motivating his staff. And it paid off. "Our vision evolved, and before long we created a reputation for outstanding customer service. The Four Seasons name itself has become a far greater asset than any bricks and mortar we could ever own."[2]

Apparently so. His leadership skills and philosophy of a "culture of mutual respect" resulted in one of the most successful hotel chains in history, with more than eighty-two hotels worldwide at last count. In 2008, Four Seasons Hotels and Resorts was once again the top choice for U.S. travellers and was named the number one hotel chain in the Zagat World's Top Hotels survey.

It is not just customers who are flocking to the hotels. When the Four Seasons announced that it was opening a new hotel in Silicon

Valley, the company received more than 3,000 applications for 300 available positions. In 2006 alone, more than 40,000 people worldwide applied to work at Four Seasons hotels.

Hmmm... maybe, just maybe, Sharp was on to something with that Golden Rule culture?

Every year, *Fortune* magazine publishes a list of the best employers to work for. Unlike many other "best company" lists, the *Fortune* list is based on employee input. The survey randomly selects employees who work in Fortune 500 companies and asks them to rate their employers on a number of factors, including credibility, communication, respect, fairness, diversity and camaraderie.

Four Seasons Hotels was on *Fortune* magazine's "100 best companies to work for" list for the eleventh time in 2008. The firm is also considered an "All Star" company by the magazine for being one of only fourteen organizations that have been on the list every year since it launched in 1998.

Why are Four Seasons employees – chamber maids, bell hops and waiters – so happy to be working at Four Seasons? What causes employees to line up to work at the hotel? What factor is responsible for the average fifteen-year term of service among senior executives and general managers?

According to Nick Mutton, executive vice president of human resources, it is the workplace culture. "We have worked very hard to build a culture where our people feel as respected and cared for as our guests..."[3]

At the Four Seasons, the Golden Rule has never been a paper strategy. It is a deeply felt ethical belief shared by everyone in the corporation, from senior management through to the front line and around the world, regardless of nationality. "It allows us to treat each other, as well as our guests, with an extra measure of caring and thoughtfulness... We will treat every employee with dignity and respect, and strive to be fair and just."[4]

In 2006, Sharp sold the Four Seasons hotel chain for $3.4 billion. His personal share from the employee incentive plan netted him $288 million. He chose to stay on as CEO of the hotel chain, as did his second in command, president and COO Kathleen Taylor. After more than forty years, Sharp still walks the talk of respect. He spends time every working day talking with employees at one of the many Four Seasons hotels.

A Paper Strategy – Talking Is a Lot Easier than Walking

We are all familiar with the Golden Rule. In my training sessions, we talk about defining respect and the Golden Rule is always mentioned. Participants discuss it and the unspoken message is, "This is pretty obvious, isn't it? We already know this!"

In fact, while we may all know about the Golden Rule , many of us don't live by it. Few workplaces actually reflect the Golden Rule in their workplace culture. At best, it's just a paper strategy.

Lots of organizations have impressive mission, vision and values statements. Many contain language about mutual respect, empowerment and equal treatment. But the corporate culture that employees actually experience often differs from the beautifully framed prints of company values so prominently displayed.

A number of years ago I was hired on to deal with an allegation of harassment involving a manager and one of her direct reports. While gathering background information, I learned that this manager had a history of harassment complaints against her. I also learned that, despite that history, this manager had recently been promoted.

When I arrived at the worksite, I was directed to a large boardroom where I set up the first interview. Partway through the interview I noticed a poster that covered almost half of one the walls. It was the organization's mission statement. It talked about the Golden Rule, promoting respect of both employees and clients, and about the intention of the organization to support and nurture this concept.

The words in the poster implied that this was a great place to work, but my investigation was revealing that the departmental manager's bullying, and the failure of the employer to do anything about that, made it a severely toxic work environment.

I sat in that room day after day, gathering evidence to substantiate the hostile and negative working environment in her department. The employer had been made aware of the manager's behaviour on numerous occasions by a number of employees. It had been going on for years.

Whenever I had a break between interviews, I looked up at that huge mission statement and was struck by the irony. The poster looked impressive, but it offered just words on a board. The words meant nothing here.

Midway through the investigation, the woman who had filed the complaint quit her job. By all accounts, she was good at her job and a valuable long-term employee. She was bright and ambitious and had been moving up in the ranks. Her former manager described her as energetic and diligent, an individual who had added a lot to her team. She had been sorry to lose her.

The employee called me to let me know her decision. She confided that other organizations had been making her offers for a while but she had really wanted to stay where she was. She was loyal to the organization, liked her work and had been happy working there – until three years earlier when she had applied for and received a promotion that resulted in her reporting directly to the "bullying" manager.

She'd finally been convinced to leave by the fact that my investigation was unlikely to have any effect. Although she'd filed a harassment complaint under the corporate policy, the complaint involved personal harassment, also known as workplace bullying. As upcoming chapters will reveal, not all types of harassment complaints are equal. In most provinces in Canada and in the U.S., there is currently no legal obligation for an employer to deal with a complaint of workplace bullying. I had already explained to this employee that regardless of my findings, at the end of the day, if the employer decided to do nothing about it, that would be the end of the line. She would have no legal recourse unless she quit and filed a complaint of constructive dismissal, which would be expensive and exhausting. That, for her, was the straw that broke the camel's back.

As an investigator, I have the power to conduct a thorough fact-finding investigation. The employer has to agree to my terms of reference, and I can choose for whom I consult, but I have no power to influence what happens after I deliver my report.

The departing employee had been telling management about the problem for over a year. Their consistent response was that it was a personality conflict and she needed to work it out. However, her attempt to approach it that way had only made things worse. Her manager's response had been consistent: The employee was the problem and if she wasn't happy, she should transfer out.

The employee had filed the complaint as a last resort, thinking that the employer would be forced to act. When she learned that the type of harassment she was experiencing was not a legal issue for the employer – that she had no legal recourse to ensure that the situation was addressed – she gave up. She contacted another company and told them she was ready to make the change.

This organization talked the talk but did not walk the walk.

It's easy to develop a mission and vision statement, or hold a retreat to develop corporate values. It's easy to phone someone like me to come in and write a Respectful Workplace policy. Companies can get a complete set of Respectful Workplace Behavioural Guidelines and a thorough policy. But none of this converts the culture, prompts would-be employees to line up to work for the firm or gets it into "The Fortune 100 Best Companies to Work For" list.

Building a respectful workplace culture requires commitment – real, long-term, commitment. It requires a commitment to action based upon "a deeply felt ethical belief, shared by everyone in the corporation…"[5] This belief must be initiated, promoted and sustained by those in power in the organization.

Ultimately, it comes down to the dynamic of power. It comes down to who has the power, and what choices those who have it make.

Building a respectful culture is work. It can be hard, scary, messy, uncomfortable work, and not just for a few, but for many in the workplace. It requires honesty and disclosure. It requires confronting fear and prejudice. It requires change – in some cases, deep, profound change, both personal and organizational.

One of the fundamental changes involves a shift in the balance of power. A respectful workplace is an empowered workplace where employees follow a direction because they respect their leaders and are committed to promoting the clearly communicated goals of the organization. They feel connected and valued and know that their unique contribution is adding to their team and organization's success.

A leader in a respectful workplace culture is not threatened by employees who show talent and promise. Such a leader supports them so they thrive and excel, even if that means they become a peer rather than subordinate. An enlightened leader leads by inclusion and example, not by bullying and threatening.

That kind of empowerment can be pretty scary for some people in positions of power. North American culture encourages us to interpret everything as black and white, win or lose. More for one means less for the other. "If he/she gets more power, that must mean I will have less." Some people are reluctant to give away their power. Let's face it, the "have-nots" want to become the "haves." It's not the other way around.

Lots of companies with impressive mission statements participate in the *Fortune* magazine survey but never get close to the Top 100. Why? Often because those in positions of power don't really understand the importance of adopting respect as a core organizational value. In other cases, those leaders lack the will or drive to do the work necessary to build a respectful workplace culture. They are unwilling to make the painful decisions required or fearful of what might happen if they do.

The win/lose paradigm creates that fear. But just because employees are empowered doesn't mean they will aim to become CEO. In a respectful workplace culture, empowerment means supporting each employee's aspiration, based on his or her talents and capabilities. In this way, an organization can truly tap into the wealth of opportunities that respectful management of difference provides.

As the Four Seasons hotel chain and other Employers of Choice featured throughout this book illustrate, respect and empowerment means business success. The Respectful Workplace scenario is a win/win paradigm. Both the business and the employees who work there succeed.

This type of culture can develop only when a leader chooses, as Sharp did, to commit to the Road to Respect.

2

Do You Know Where Your Culture Is?

Organization culture is like pornography; it is hard to define, but you know it when you see it.

—ELLEN WALLACH

A T A RECENT Vancouver Board of Trade networking event, I met a young woman who had been chosen to participate in the Leaders of Tomorrow mentoring program. This program selects outstanding students and tries to "bridge the gap between students' school and career experience, and accelerate their professional success in the business community."[1]

When she asked me what I did for a living, I responded with my sound bite: "I am in the business of promoting human dignity in the workplace. I work with employers to create respectful workplaces, workplaces where employees feel included, safe and valued as individuals."

"Wow," she responded. "I wish I had met you last summer. I had a summer job I thought was going to be just great. It seemed like a winner company and a fabulous opportunity for me. But after I started, I found the atmosphere there really awful. I mean, everyone was really nice on the surface, but underneath it was all gossiping and backstabbing. Conflict everywhere. I just couldn't stand it."

This young woman was charismatic, bright and ambitious. She had been chosen by the Board of Trade for her impressive credentials. Being a "millennial" (individuals born in the 1980s and 1990s, also referred to as Gen Y), she was probably also community minded, action oriented and interested in team-based relationships.

She was the type of person most organizations are keen to attract and retain. However, she told me straight out that she would have quit had this not been a summer-only job. She had decided she simply didn't fit in. In this case, the organization had been able to attract but not retain an impressive young woman.

The organization probably had inspiring mission, vision and values statements. The student came in expecting those core values to be reflected in the corporate culture, and was surprised and disappointed to find that was not the case. As we have already learned, the corporate culture that employees experience often differs from the one defined in a company's public statements.

Corporate culture is critical to business success. It consistently determines whether an employee is engaged, productive and connected to the workplace – and whether an employee decides to stay. Research has established a direct link between corporate culture, employee performance and organizational profitability. A Harvard Business School study of more than 200 organizations showed that corporate culture significantly impacted long-term economic performance and that culture could enhance or detract from performance depending on the culture's characteristics.[2]

The Four Seasons Hotel chain, IBM, Southwest Airlines and Google are just a few examples of firms that credit their success to their workplace culture strategies.

So, what is organizational or workplace culture? Workplace culture is the personality of the organization. It is the answer you get when you ask, "What's it like to work here?" It is what employees are referring to when they say, "Around here we don't do it that way," or "This is how we do things here."

I hear these statements all the time when I am talking to employees. "This company just doesn't support its supervisors." "This company doesn't deal with issues; it just moves people to different departments." "Gossip is a way of life around here." "You have to put up with that kind of stuff if you are going to work here. I don't care anymore. I just come in and do my job and go home."

Workplace culture is the shared attitudes, beliefs and values that influence behaviour and shape the experiences of employees. Workplace culture determines how people feel about the place they work.

Every organization has a distinct culture. That is how it should be. Improving workplace culture is not about creating cookie-cutter companies. Workplace culture varies according to organizational size, business history, the type of work, the variety of tasks and jobs involved, who does the work, how the work is structured, if it is unionized, its location and, last but certainly not least, leadership practices and style.

Sometimes culture is the product of a deliberate strategy. Sometimes it evolves on its own. Allowing organizational culture to evolve on its own is a risky business. That is definitely not the approach I recommend. None of the outstanding companies featured in this book left organizational culture to chance. All took deliberate action to shape workplace culture. While each is engaged in a very different type of business, they all made purposeful choices about workplace culture and adopted respect as a core organizational value. The other commonality is what that purposeful choice produced: profitability and recognition as an Employer of Choice.

Who's Got the Power?

Workplace culture and organizational power are intricately interwoven. While I don't subscribe to a Machiavellian approach to power, I have come to appreciate the critical importance of power and the need to make appropriate choices from that perspective. Just as there can be a disconnect between stated core values and the actual workplace culture, so too can there be a disconnect between the organizational chart and who really wields power in an organization.

I learned this lesson when I worked in the labour relations department of an international airline. Although the unions did not appear anywhere on the corporate organizational chart, it did not take me long to realize the immense power they wielded. There was also the matter of gender and power. I soon learned that while the women who reported to men in power did not technically have positional power, they gained power by association. Their power came from knowing and being connected to powerful people. If I wanted to meet with our departmental vice president, I had to go through his executive assistant. If she liked me, it was much easier to get access to the VP. If she didn't like me, somehow his schedule was always booked up.

I also learned about the power that workplace bullies can wield. As I was investigating a complaint of sexual harassment, I learned that all the employees in the department, including the supervisors and the union reps, were intimidated by two people named in the complaint. These two had personal power as the result of being big men who used their physical size to intimidate those around them. They made it a point to talk about how many people they had threatened and allegedly beaten up over the weekend. They talked openly about enjoying pornography. They intimidated other employees into doing their own work, threatening violence to anyone who challenged them. No one in the department would take them on. That is, until a new female employee started working in the department.

This woman had grown up in a country filled with violence. She was familiar with victimization and the abuse of power. She was not about to put up with the kind of inappropriate behaviour she had left her homeland to escape. When the two men started making inappropriate comments to her, she filed a complaint.

During the ensuing investigation, her car tires were slashed and she received threatening phone calls at home. The police had to get involved. But this woman wouldn't back down. She remained brave and courageous until she got what she knew she and her co-workers deserved – a safe and respectful workplace. As a result of her commitment, the truth was finally revealed about what had been going on in that department. The company and the union both supported this woman, and the two men were escorted off the worksite and dismissed.

What's Respect Got to Do with It?
An Overview of Canadian Human Rights Law

So, was that woman right? Do we all deserve – indeed, have the right to expect – a safe and respectful workplace? The answer to that is a resounding yes. Just as we have laws in Canada requiring employers to be vigilant about providing a safe workplace, we have laws that require employers to provide a "respectful" workplace.

How did this notion of respect find its way into the sphere of employment? In 1948, the United Nations adopted the Universal Declaration of Human Rights, the first document in human history that formally recognized the notion that all of us, by virtue of our membership in the human family, deserve respectful and dignified treatment. The Universal Declaration also stressed the importance of enshrining these human rights in law.

What the Universal Declaration didn't do was explicitly define respectful and dignified treatment. It left that up to the individual nation states that were supposed to pass laws to promote such treatment.

In Canada, we took the Universal Declaration pretty seriously, perhaps because the author of that document, John Peter Humphrey, hailed from the province of New Brunswick. We started passing legislation to define and promote respectful and dignified treatment in Canada almost before the ink was dry.

By 1985 we'd enshrined a definition of respectful treatment in the Equality section, Section 15, of the Canadian Charter of Rights and Freedoms. The Charter, adopted in 1982, is former Prime Minister Pierre Trudeau's legacy to Canadians.

The Charter is a visionary and cultural document that defines and promotes the type of culture Canadians want: one that is tolerant, fair, just and mutually respectful.

The Charter is a document that provides direction to our legislators. The theory is that Canadian law translates the values of tolerance, fairness, justice and mutual respect into actual experience for you and me in Canadian society. Not that easy to do when you think about how big and diverse this country is, and the fact that we are divided up into provinces that also have a role to play in the translation of these values. And then there is the issue of power, how it is distributed and manifested within a democratic system. Yikes! Translating those values throughout society in the whole country sounds like a pretty daunting task.

On the other hand it should be much easier to translate those values in a workplace. The difference, one that is clearly recognized in law, is the issue of power. In a workplace it is the employer who is supposed to have the power.

The Charter of Rights and Freedoms is the foundation of Canadian law. Section 15, which is the Equality section, the section from which all our Human Rights laws in Canada flow, is considered "quasi-constitutional." That means it takes precedence over other branches of the law. To use a metaphor, if the Charter of Rights is the foundation, then Human Rights laws are the ground floor. Practically speaking, you need to go through the ground floor before you can get to other floors.

Consequently, equality (this notion of respectful and dignified treatment) is really a core value for us in Canada. Our legislators have set up our legal system purposefully. They made a deliberate choice to promote a respectful culture and embrace mutual respect as a core value.

Our lawmakers made another deliberate choice. The law is specific about just what aspects of our culture need to be concerned about respectful and dignified treatment: employment, provision of goods and services, and housing. This means that if you are an employer, you have a statutory obligation to provide a respectful and dignified working environment for your employees.

Here is a hot tip for you. Statutory obligation means an obligation you can't get out of. It's not a "nice to have if you feel like it" type of commitment. It means you are required to do it, and on the hook if an employee decides you are not doing it. One of the main reasons for statutory obligation is that courts recognize the theoretical power equation that exists in most workplaces. The employer has power and the employee does not. The law exists to help equalize that power differential.

We take a closer look at Human Rights laws in upcoming chapters. For the moment, let's focus on what this notion of statutory obligation means for you as an employer. Practically translated, the law requires you to have a policy about respectful behaviours as defined by law. This policy has to include a complaint mechanism for employees who believe that their rights are being violated. And since no one will know about their rights and what to do if they are violated unless you tell them, the subtext is that an employer will need to provide some training. You need to make sure employees know their rights and responsibilities relative to your human rights policy. That policy should be a summary and restatement of the applicable human rights statute. A company's human rights policy, like the law, exists to empower the employee.

The other important fact is that while the law refers to respectful and dignified treatment, our law defines those terms in a very narrow manner. Simply put, Section 15 says that respectful treatment means non-discriminatory treatment. If you are being discriminated against, then you are not being treated respectfully. Thus, Canadian culture is respectful if people are not being discriminated against. By extension, a non-discriminatory workplace is a respectful workplace.

Your workplace human rights policy can be compared to the human rights statutes in general. Human rights laws always start with a broad proactive purpose statement that refers to fostering a respectful society. In fact, however, our laws are used in a reactive manner. Most of our human rights bodies focus very little on proactive issues. Rather they are almost totally occupied with the reactive side – the complaint side.

If we have a problem, we can file a complaint and eventually get our "day in court." Sometimes the remedy that the court metes out alludes to putting measures in place to ensure the creation of a respectful workplace for the person complaining. This really means culture change. The complaint has revealed a disrespectful workplace. The remedy is to transform that disrespectful workplace into a respectful workplace for the individual complaining. In theory, a disrespectful workplace culture will be transformed into a respectful workplace culture. It all sounds good.

In practice, however, it doesn't always work out that way. The courts' power is easily thwarted if those in positions of power choose to preserve their existing culture and resist cultural change.

Take the case of Michael McKinnon. McKinnon started working as a correctional officer in Toronto's Metro East Detention Centre in 1977. McKinnon is aboriginal, but his ethnicity is not obvious. He looks like a white man. He soon found the Toronto area jail an overtly racist environment in which to work. There were lots of inappropriate comments made about aboriginals. McKinnon advised his employer that he was aboriginal and that he found the comments offensive.

Not only did that fail to stop the comments, but McKinnon now found himself on the receiving end of a constant barrage of racist behaviour. He was asked if he was having a pow wow. His co-workers donned feather Indian headdresses and initiated war cries when he entered the room. He was referred to as the f__ing Indian, Wagon Burner, Geronimo, Tomahawk, Crazy Horse and other such names. His wife also worked in the detention centre. Although she was not aboriginal, she was referred to as Squaw McKinnnon. McKinnon was publicly humiliated in front of inmates and had favorable assignments taken away from him.

He put up with the behaviour for a number of years before filing a complaint. In 1998, the Ontario Human Rights Tribunal found that he had suffered discrimination. His employer was ordered to stop the discrimination and create a respectful environment. However, things got worse. Both McKinnon and his wife suffered retaliation as soon as others in the workplace knew he had filed his first complaint. He filed two subsequent complaints. Each time, legal decisions supported him; the courts were clear that both McKinnon and his wife were working in a poisoned work environment. The Tribunal even presented a specific list of remedies. Each time, the employer chose not to implement them.

After the third complaint, both McKinnon and his wife were placed on paid leave while the Ministry was ordered to address the poisoned, disrespectful work culture. Rather than admit any liability, or even acknowledge the type of workplace culture which the complaints had clearly substantiated, the Ministry of Correctional Services (McKinnon's employer) chose to ignore the orders yet again, and filed appeals to get the decisions reversed. The Ministry chose to keep both McKinnon and his wife out of the workplace and pay them full wages for eight years rather than acknowledge that the workplace culture in the correctional system was inherently disrespectful.

Eighteen years after his original complaint, on January 30, 2007, another decision came down supporting McKinnon's claim of discrimination. The 300-page decision severely criticized the Ministry for "shameful" conduct. The Tribunal found that it had buried complaints from McKinnon or investigated them in an incompetent manner, and that it had financially and morally supported employees who had been found guilty of human rights violations.

When I read about the case, I could only wonder at the Ministry of Corrections' choices. Were they all a bunch of ignorant racists? Did they really hate either McKinnon, his wife or all aboriginals that much? I don't think so. I don't even think race was the crucial issue here. To start to understand what was going on at the Metro East Detention Centre, I think we need to ponder prison culture's core values. We need to think about power and how it manifests in such a culture. And we need to think about the fear raised when the values of that culture are fundamentally challenged.

A prison, like many other organizations, reflects a militaristic command and control model. It is based on the win/lose paradigm, the "us" versus "them" philosophy followed in war, corporate life and sports for generations. Bullying and conformity are accepted managerial practices, condoned and rewarded. The culture emphasizes strength, competition and winning. You are expected to be tough, to give as good as you get. You are either one of "us," or you are not. And when you're not, then anything, and any tactic, is fair game.

This cultural belief system is often accepted by employees in traditional male-dominated work environments. Staff don't complain about name-calling, harassment and jokes.

"It's what we do and how it is here. If you can't take that, you shouldn't be working here. Sure we tell off-colour jokes and call each other derogatory nicknames. We all do it. You've gotta have a thick hide if you are going to work here."

From my perspective, McKinnon's complaint called into question the entire value system on which the workplace culture was based. Had the Ministry admitted to harassment, the floodgates would have opened, washing away the very underpinning of the Toronto East Detention Centre culture. That outcome was simply too threatening to contemplate.

McKinnon looked like a white man. They thought he was one of them. And if he wasn't one of them, it wasn't a big deal, as long as he was prepared to play by the rules. When McKinnon made it clear that he wasn't interested in playing by the rules, he in effect declared war. And war was what he got. It became winner take all and they tried to beat him down. Rather than look at the behaviour McKinnon was complaining about, which was the real problem, the Ministry chose to discount the behaviour and focus on McKinnon himself as the problem.

I don't for a second believe that the Ministry of Correctional services sat down and made a decision to adopt this fundamentally disrespectful and toxic workplace culture and its underlying values. It was a culture that grew on its own. Had McKinnon not blown the whistle, it would have continued to flourish regardless of Charter of Rights and Human Rights laws.

It is important in life to see things as they are. Toxic workplace cultures exist. Historical discrimination is a reality that affects our workplaces. The command and control model of leadership is alive and well in many corporate cultures. It is crucial that we recognize the fundamental legacy of power-based behaviours in all North American businesses. In some cases abusive and disrespectful practices produce subcultures that flourish unbeknownst to those in human resources or the executive offices.

Discrimination, harassment and bullying are all related to power. Research on workplace bullying shows that in most cases, one individual holds power over the other.[3] When there is inconsistency in leadership styles, when someone with power can manage by intimidation and fear, the result is often a command and control subculture.

Since leadership style is the single greatest influence on workplace culture, variations in leadership styles and practices often produce a cultural disconnect. Rather than a cohesive culture – one that remains consistent throughout the organization regardless of the position or department in which an employee works – many organizations are collections of disparate subcultures.

I learned about this firsthand when I worked at an airline. I will never forget my first day of work there. I had retired from my life as a professional dancer just two weeks prior to starting a job as a labour relations specialist. My new boss took me on a tour of the huge worksite and I felt like I had landed on Mars. I had spent most of my adult life either in school or surrounded by creative people who actively expressed their passion at work. Everyone I met that day seemed formal and conservative, making me feel like I was in a foreign environment.

After the tour, my boss brought me back to my windowless office, plunked a huge pile of files on my desk and told me to review them.

I sat at that desk in a complete panic. What had I done, accepting this job? I was going to have to sit at a desk for hours. As a dancer, I had sat only when I was watching a rehearsal or performance. I felt I could not survive another second in this job.

I took a deep breath and forced myself to calm down. I had taken this job to gain experience – experience I would use to start my own consulting business. I would have to suffer some short-term pain for long-term gain. So I pulled the first file off the pile and started reading.

I worked at the airline for six years and as it turned out, most of that time I could not have asked for a better learning opportunity. I reported to a wonderful director who became a mentor, role model and friend. As my life changed, I found I had things in common with my co-workers. While I never fully fit in with the corporate or departmental culture, I learned to adapt and accept my role.

Then in 1997, my director called me while I was on maternity leave to offer me a new position as the corporate human rights advisor. While I loved my eight-month-old daughter with every fibre of my being, the thought of focusing on something other than baby food and laundry certainly appealed to me. When my boss promised I could return to work on a gradual basis and place my daughter in on-site daycare, I couldn't refuse.

I'd been back at work less than five minutes when I realized the new position was a perfect fit. I discovered a passion for human rights work that I had never felt for labour work. Maybe this was my intended path, I reflected. For several months, then, I found myself engaged in work I loved with my daughter nearby. I was even situated in the same office, reporting to a great boss and working with co-workers I liked and respected.

Then my boss told me there had been some discussion about my new position. I was to submit a written summary of my duties and note where I thought the position should be situated on the corporate organizational chart. I was pleased to provide this input; the request felt respectful and useful.

But months passed with no word on the document I had

submitted. No one involved me in any conversations about it. Then one day my director told me I would now be reporting both to her and a director in the human resources department. Although it irked me that I had spent time on a document that had clearly been ignored, I raised no objection. And for several months, not much changed. For the most part, I was my own boss. I did interact with my new boss on rare occasions, but went to my director in the labour department when I had questions. I knew her; I trusted and respected her input.

But one day my director informed me that a new department was being created within human resources, and I was being moved into it. Rather than reporting to two directors, I would be reporting to a newly hired manager. I was sad to lose my boss and mentor, and miffed to have to report to a manager rather than director. It felt like a demotion.

My new manager informed me that other staff were being transferred into the department and we'd soon be moving into a new area: an old data entry room currently filled with boxes and old furniture. A few weeks later, I received an email that was short and to the point: the labour department had hired someone to replace me and I would need to vacate my office within a week.

I was furious. I was being summarily kicked out of where I had worked for six years. Why had no one taken the time to tell me in person? While it had been some time since I'd been a member of the labour department, I had been working there for a long time. I approached my new manager in human resources to ask her where I would be moving. She informed me I'd be working in a cubicle. I objected, stressing the confidential nature of my job; I conducted sensitive interviews with emotional people involved in harassment complaints. My new manager seemed to understand. She requested an office for me. But given the firm's command and control culture, this involved a lengthy, bureaucratic decision-making process. During that process, senior management discovered and informed me that my new position had been classified at a lower pay grade and did not qualify for an office. The belated discovery of the pay grade meant I could remain at my current pay, which as it turned out was the same as my new manager – a fact that in itself set up an interesting power dynamic.

I was told that multiple levels of approval were needed to grant an office to someone at my position's pay grade. It all seemed ridiculous to me. What did pay grade or location or to whom I reported have to do with anything? I was concerned about my work. Surely someone could find me an office to protect the privacy and dignity of people involved in harassment complaints? I was flabbergasted at this turn of events. I felt like I was working for a new company.

It didn't take long for matters to disintegrate completely. My manager told me she had tried but there was nothing more she could do. The HR director had approved the office but senior executives had not agreed. I would have to work out of a cubicle. I continued to express my concerns. She suggested I conduct interviews in the cafeteria. I regarded this as ludicrous. The employees with whom I met were often emotionally distressed, traumatized, angry – and they often divulged confidential information about fellow workers. Anyone overhearing us in the cafeteria would know I was the company's human rights specialist.

It finally dawned on me that I was in trouble. I could hear it in my boss's tone. I was becoming a problem. I needed to move into my cubicle and stop making trouble. In retrospect, I can appreciate her perspective. She was new to the organization.

However, I would not give in. I asked my manager if I could try to obtain permission on my own and she said yes. With her permission, I made an appointment with the newly appointed vice president of human resources, a long-time employee I knew through my labour work.

The new VP told me she would look into it, but just hours later, my manager confronted me angrily. She berated me for going to speak to the VP. What was my problem? Why couldn't I accept the fact that I was not going to get an office?

I told her I'd been under the impression she'd agreed I could pursue the matter, which she denied. She was furious that I had gone over her head. "What are you trying to do to me?" She advised me that she was going to go to the VP and let her know this had all been dealt with through the appropriate channels and not to take any action to resolve the issue.

I stood there in a state of shock. Despite a career in labour/management conflict, I'd just seen my skills evaporate when confronted personally. This issue had become personal. My request for an office was no longer the problem. My insisting that I needed an office was the problem. I was the problem.

Suddenly, I understood. The issue was never going to be resolved. I was going to have to do my job in the cubicle, and hold private, sensitive, emotional interviews in semi-public places. I could not do that. With a sinking feeling, I realized the only option left to me was to quit.

I have seen this over and over in my consulting practice. Letting an issue get personal is what tends to derail a process. This is why communication courses emphasize the importance of separating the person from the problem. A problem can remain impersonal; a person cannot. A problem can be resolved; a person cannot.

During my six years at this company, I'd formed my impression of the organizational culture while in the labour department – an entity in which individuals were segmented according to which union they dealt with. My director, unlike this HR manager to whom I now reported, was a savvy, action-oriented leader who was passionate about and supportive of her employees. Early on in my career, she told me she "knew how things worked around here." She had no patience for long decision making, so she always found a way to make things happen for the good of both the employees and department. She'd been the one to approve my returning to work on a gradual basis; she'd done the same for two other new mothers. Never mind that there was no official policy for part time or job sharing. Knowing I was a nursing mother, she'd offered me the human rights portfolio because it involved less travelling. She always went to bat for employees without making a big deal about it.

After the altercation with my new manager, I sought out my

former boss. She was upset, angry and empathetic, but powerless to help me, since I was now in a different division. I was alone, without an advocate. I no longer had a supportive boss I could trust, or colleagues I knew and respected.

The next day I moved my files to the space where my cubicle, I was told, would soon be built. For now, it lacked partitions, but my manager told me cheerily they'd soon be there. I felt humiliated, de-valued, angry and sad. At that point I did what many individuals in similar situation do. I visited my doctor and obtained a note for a two-week medical leave.

When I returned, I found my boss polite but distant. I felt completely uncomfortable around her. Soon after my return she advised me in writing that my hours would be by the rule book – none of my former flexibility. I told myself I would try to work under these circumstances, but during the course of each work day, I found myself whispering during phone conversations with clients, and checking to see who might be listening. I worried about leaving files out and unlocked. During one interview, for which I managed to borrow an office, I was quoting office policy to the client when the words hit home: "The company is committed to providing you with a respectful work environment." I stopped and hurried on to explain the next steps in the process.

I went home that evening and told my husband I had to quit my job. I could not quote a policy that didn't seem to apply to me. It felt hypocritical. I no longer believed it. It was time, I told him, to start my consulting business.

The next day I submitted my written resignation and proceeded to make rounds to say goodbye to co-workers. Many said, "Wow, you are so lucky." Lucky, I wondered. What did luck have to do with it? I had made a risky choice, especially given that my husband was also self-employed and we had a two-year-old. We were losing financial security, our extended medical and dental, our life insurance and flight benefits.

Thinking back, however, I understand their comments. The airline's survival had always seemed precarious. Employees were bombarded with dire financial news, takeover threats, pay cuts and more pay cuts. The unions held enormous power and management was pretty beaten down. Managers had not had a raise in years; they put in long hours and most had seen their salaries erode over time. They often supervised unionized staff who made significantly more money than they did. Everyone grumbled and complained. The downtrodden atmosphere was something I had grown to accept. It was just the way it was there.

But to my mind, it wasn't the industry that dictated these conditions; it was the choices executives were making in response to the conditions. They did not adopt a culture that would empower employees. We all knew we were in a battle to save our airline, but the culture did not encourage employees to think like winners. Everyone felt vulnerable and fearful. The underlying message was that we should be happy we still had a job.

In Richard Wright's novel *Native Son*, the African-American writer's main character, Bigger Thomas, says, "The impulse to dream has been slowly beaten out of me through the experience of life."[4]

When continually bombarded with a message that says you are not worth much, you start to believe it. Any organization with a negative, pessimistic or disrespectful culture erodes an individual's sense of self-worth. Your perception of who you are becomes your prison – you are locked into a fear-based mindset.

When I quit my job, I freed myself from that sense of being trapped rather than empowered. Had I stayed working in that cubicle, I'd be a different person today: unhappy, resentful, no longer optimistic with a strong sense of values and a passion for life.

When individuals feel trapped and victimized, the result is a workplace phenomenon called "presenteeism." We all know what absenteeism is. Absenteeism occurs when an employee is physically away from work. Increased absenteeism is one effect of disrespectful behaviour at work.

Absenteeism is costing Canadian employers $8.6 billion annually. Presenteeism, which occurs when an employee is still physically at work, but not really present in any meaningful sense, has been calculated as costing Canadian employers up to twice that amount.[5] Employees are not engaged, focused, motivated or even interested in their job anymore. They just show up and put in the minimum effort required

This type of mentality does not produce successful businesses. The type of culture that encourages presenteeism and absenteeism does not enable a business to survive when the going gets tough. It evolves when leaders fail to strategically build a culture, instead allowing organizational culture to develop on its own. It exists when individuals in positions of power fail to appreciate the link between workplace culture, job performance and profit.

So, now you have to make a choice. Which outcome do you choose? Are you going to use your power to build a respectful and successful workplace culture? Or allow your culture to evolve on its own and take your chances on the outcome?

Behind door number one is the choice to engage in a purposeful strategy.

Behind door number two is the choice to leave things to chance.

If you choose door number two, you may as well put this book down or give it away. This book is not for you.

If you choose door number one, you are someone prepared to take action. Congratulations. You are taking the first step on the Road to Respect. You are embarking on a journey to build a respectful workplace culture, a culture that can propel you to become an Employer of Choice on the Path to Profit. Read on.

3

The Good, the Bad and the Ugly –
Respect, Assumptions and Prejudice

Not everything that is faced can be changed, but nothing can be changed until it is faced.

—JAMES BALDWIN

CONGRATULATIONS! You chose door number one and are ready to build a respectful workplace culture. Before you go any further, however, you should know what you are getting into. Deciding to adopt respect as a core value in your organizational culture means being prepared to take a brutally honest look at both yourself and your workplace. You will, in all likelihood, have to step out of your comfort zone. Creating a respectful workplace culture requires a commitment to talk about and deal with difficult issues like prejudice, stereotyping, racism, sexism, equality, inclusion, language, communication, conflict, fear and power. Definitely not topics that many people relish discussing.

I know it is not "acceptable" to be prejudiced. No reasonable person admits they are. I certainly didn't think I had prejudices. As a human rights practitioner, I work to educate people on the evils of discrimination and discriminatory harassment. I have always believed I need to lead by example. I have made a conscious effort to be open and curious about others, and to force myself to challenge stereotypes and assumptions.

I do a fair amount of training in my consulting practice. I love training. I have a performing arts background and training is a kind of performance – one with lots of improvisation. I never know what someone might say or do, so I have to be ready to respond in a way that connects with them and illuminates the topic. I have to be dynamic, responsive and "on my toes" in order to deliver an effective and powerful session.

When I first started conducting human rights training, I often found myself in traditionally male-dominated workplaces. This never bothered me. As a labour relations practitioner, I'd worked with a male-dominated union. I was used to dealing with groups of men and thought I was prepared for whatever would come my way.

Early on in my career I'd learned the importance of conscious clothing choices. A male colleague and I were setting up for a training session when, knowing he'd gone out for drinks the night before with participants from the previous day's session, I asked him if he had useful feedback.

"Oh yeah," he said with an impish grin. "They loved it! Man, they couldn't stop talking about it."

"Huh?" I asked suspiciously. "Topic's too dry to get anyone excited. What do you mean, they couldn't stop talking about it?"

He looked me right in the eye and said "Your t_ts! They couldn't stop talking about how the course really picked up after you took off your jacket."

I turned a bright shade of pink. "Men," I muttered, and turned my back to continue setting up. These were business people who were supposed to be discussing an important organizational issue and instead they were focused on my chest!

Of course, it was easier to pretend I'd shrugged off the comment than to actually stop thinking about it. As a former dancer, I'd always taken my body for granted. I did a quick visual recap of my actions the previous day. The room had grown hot. I'd removed my jacket, under which I'd worn a neutral silk shell – nothing low cut, tight or revealing. Call me naïve, but until that moment I had not realized that taking off my jacket in a room full of men would be a problem. I resolved to accomplish what I'd arrived to do: keep participants focused on the material I was delivering. If that meant keeping my jacket on regardless of room temperature, so be it.

I've stuck with that policy ever since. What didn't occur to me at the time was the disrespect my colleague had shown in smirking as he shared the information with me, and in presumably being part of the conversation the evening before, rather than in any way trying to squelch it. By not responding to that aspect of the conversation, I realize in retrospect that I missed an opportunity to question the existing culture and underlying values that encouraged that behaviour.

Soon after I started consulting, I had to come to grips with the fact that many participants at my training sessions were resistant to the idea of a respectful workplace, especially those in the white male demographic. And with growing frequency, that's the audience I found myself addressing. As someone who loves a challenge, I constantly reworked my material to deal with issues and perspectives my participants brought up. I was determined to be effective, compelling and inspiring, and judging from feedback forms, I was moving in the right direction.

However, I began to understand what I was up against when I was contracted to train municipal firefighters. During days of sessions training over 300 firefighters, I saw only a handful of women and visible minorities. It was a sea of friendly white male faces. And they were friendly. For the first few days, I thought things were going well. Then a participant decided to challenge me on the issue of female firefighters. "They can't do the job. Don't you know that there are different standards for female firefighters?" he asked.

"Well, that's not how the law is supposed to be interpreted," I began. "The standards might change to make sure no group is being inadvertently disadvantaged. But job requirements have to match the job, and have to be the same for everyone."

Well, did that ever get people going! Lots of men jumped in, talking all at once, saying women firefighters (none of whom I could see in the room) get all kinds of special treatment.

"Hey!" shouted one fellow, standing up and pointing at me. "You gonna be the one to tell my wife I got killed on the job 'cause some girl who got the job just 'cause she was a girl wasn't strong enough to pull me out of a burning building?" Without pausing long enough for me to reply, he continued, "Firefighting's no place for women! And anyone who says otherwise has no idea what the job's like!"

"Yeah!" others shouted, standing excitedly and joining in the shouting match. Within seconds, I felt like the room itself had caught fire; anger and hate pulsed through the crowd, and what had started as challenge quickly deteriorated into personal attacks. I had to fight to get control of the room again, as I used every tool in my public-speaking arsenal to cool them down and hold them there the rest of my session.

Today I look back on that as one of my greatest learning experiences. As John F. Kennedy once said, "When written in Chinese, the word 'crisis' is composed of two characters. One represents danger and the other represents opportunity."

It took every ounce of courage I had to return to the fire hall the next day. But I came armed with knowledge to meet what I now expected might occur. I had called the Chief and gotten clarification on every issue that had been raised. I stayed up half the night researching related case law so that I would be able to handle whatever came up. Those firefighters had made assumptions about female firefighters without having the facts. I planned my strategy and was ready for the challenge.

Word had gotten out about the previous day's free-for-all. I could feel the men's sense of empowerment. It was me and my "respectful workplace policy" against the firefighters and their culture. Not for long however.

In addition to my usual stories, I had stories about firefighters and fire halls. I spoke with authority and knowledge about their specific job standards and the modifications that had occurred. "Did you know," I asked them, "that in the over twenty years since women had started working as firefighters, there had not been one case of anyone, either another firefighter, or a civilian, being injured or compromised because that woman had not been able to do her job? On the contrary," I told them. Women that chose to work as firefighters worked diligently to prove themselves and many had received departmental commendations.

After that session a number of the guys came up to talk to me. Many had questions they had not wanted to ask with their colleagues listening. One confided that his wife was upset now that she heard that there would be more women in the fire hall. As I drove away that day I felt rejuvenated. I knew the tide had turned. I knew that I had reached some of them. They had been listening and had started thinking about what had been discussed, about the assumptions they had been making about others on the basis of gender.

That training contract convinced me that I needed to start talking more directly about prejudice and assumptions with my clients. I had experienced how assumptions could fuel the fear that gives rise to discrimination and harassment. I started to consciously incorporate these topics into my training, particularly in traditionally male-dominated workplaces where the few women employees often raised complaints about systemic gender discrimination. Typically, in such organizations men make assumptions based on unconscious and/or well-intentioned belief systems about what women can and can't do. For example, they may believe women shouldn't do the "dirty" or heavy-lifting jobs.

Under human rights laws, employees should be able to demonstrate their ability and qualifications for doing a job. If a woman applies to do a job traditionally performed by men, she should get the same consideration as a male applicant. She should be allowed to demonstrate whether or not she can do the job. She should be given the same probationary period, the same amount of training and the same support. That is the theory. In practice, however, assumptions about what a woman can or can't do often prevent her from getting the opportunity the law states she has.

One goal of my training sessions is to examine how such assumptions may negatively affect employees in the workplace. I tell participants that these assumptions are often unconscious; we often don't realize we are making them. They are part of our belief system. Prejudice is nothing but assumptions, often based on untrue beliefs. We've all grown up with different belief systems.

My training sessions offer lively and interactive discussions designed to stimulate learning. In one session a participant explained that in the works yard, they had "pink" and "blue" jobs. All new employees, he advised us, started in the works yard. But when the company started hiring women, his boss decided to divvy up the works-yard jobs so that the women did the lighter and the men the heavier work.

Not only was this news to me, but it was news to many other participants, some of whom had been working at this plant for years. We talked about the practice. "Why did it come about? Was it fair? Was it equal? Who was being disadvantaged?" Discrimination, I reminded them, is about disadvantaging a group of employees. We focused on the fact that women never got a chance to train for the heavier jobs, which in turn affected their ability to get promotions into other departments. Then one participant pointed out that it really wasn't fair to the men, who were getting all the heavy work and were therefore more prone to back injuries. In fact, this meant both men and women were experiencing discrimination. Everyone valued that realization. We concluded that assumptions about what women can and can't do serve no one. Participants agreed that greater awareness of beliefs and assumptions, and how they affect the way people are treated at work, are important.

That night, excited about a successful day, I started preparing for the next day's training session. As usual, I scanned the participant list to see how many women would be in the group. "Great, three women!" I said aloud. Then I paused and thought, "I don't know any of these women. Why am I so happy to see three females on the list? I'm assuming the session will run smoother with women present, that they will side with me if discussion becomes contentious. Which means I'm assuming the men will be against me. These are assumptions which can fuel prejudice, the very things I'm asking participants to question. Talk about the pot calling the kettle black! I'm thinking this way and I'm an expert in the laws intended to eradicate prejudice. This is proof of how subtly it can happen."

Where and when had my women-are-allies and men-are-foes sentiment arisen? In my case, I reflected, this was not an ingrained belief inherited from childhood. Rather, my chosen work, starting with my experience at that fire hall, had caused a shift in my perceptions and my belief systems.

The next day, I shared my experience. I admitted I'd been making gender-based assumptions, which was prejudice. I shared my surprise, embarrassment and shame, and my resolve to be more aware and act differently. As I spoke, I could sense a collective sigh of relief as their apprehension about what they could or couldn't say in that room evaporated. The result was a great session with all of us involved in a truly open and honest dialogue about respect in their workplace.

That experience taught me to have more empathy for people who make assumptions, and express mistrust or contempt for people different from themselves. I now talk about the underlying fears that are often expressed as assumptions and prejudice.

I have come to believe that we are all prejudiced. Maybe not overtly, because overt prejudice is obvious and easy to condemn. Sometimes, condemning others for prejudice prompts us to congratulate ourselves on our more evolved and egalitarian perspective. However, it is the covert stuff of which we need to become more aware, because it subtly affects our behaviour. The phrase "he who casts the first stone" comes to mind.

If we are going to create a truly respectful workplace, we have to be prepared to really look at ourselves. We have to accept that even though we think we are "good people," we may be engaging in behaviour based on false assumptions about those who differ from us. These assumptions can have an inadvertent negative impact on others and how we relate to them. We have to acknowledge this fact and find the courage to talk about it. Once we are aware of our beliefs and our assumptions, we can decide whether or not those beliefs and assumptions are serving us and the people with whom we work. Until we acknowledge and talk about those beliefs, until we are ready to share those covert beliefs with co-workers, we cannot build a respectful workplace culture.

One company that made the choice to talk about hidden assumptions is KPMG. I heard Beth Wilson, a member of the executive team at KPMG, speak about diversity at a Vancouver Board of Trade luncheon in November 2006. Her message was that creating an inclusive, respectful workplace was a business imperative.

"There is the clear social reason," she stated. "It is the right thing to do. But there are also clear business reasons." Wilson's and KPMG's openness are typical characteristics of Employers of Choice: the willingness to take a brutally honest look at the firm's culture – to talk about hidden beliefs and assumptions – started at the top and worked its way down to become part of the culture at KPMG.

The KPMG Way

To deal with business realities – to be able to work with the best – we must constantly look into ourselves for those unintentional biases that cut us off from other people. It's a good human relations strategy. It's a good business strategy. Keep challenging your own perceptions.

—BETH WILSON, FCA, Canadian managing partner, KPMG LLP

KPMG LLP is known as one of Canada's leading professional services firms. Its accolades are impressive. *Maclean's* magazine recognized KPMG as one of Canada's Top 100 Employers for 2009, for the sixth time since 2001, when *Maclean's* initiated the list. KPMG was also chosen as one of Greater Toronto's Top 75 Employers for 2009. A *Canadian Business* poll of university students identified KPMG as the employer for which business graduates would most like to work.

KPMG's role is to help clients meet challenges and respond to opportunities. As the new millennium progressed, KPMG's leaders decided that the firm's biggest challenge was to attract and retain the best and brightest in an industry where competition for talent is fierce. To do that, they set a goal to be recognized as an Employer of Choice. They realized that formalizing their commitment to a respectful, diverse and inclusive workplace would give them a competitive advantage from a business perspective. So in 2003, those in power at KPMG made a choice to adopt a new business initiative to formally recognize KPMG's commitment to a respectful and inclusive work environment.

This decision was not made in reaction to a problem or complaint. KPMG was a successful firm with a good reputation. The company was not having trouble attracting new employees. It had a diverse workforce and a number of female partners. KPMG enjoyed a deliberate and values-based workplace culture. We've all heard that saying, "If it ain't broke, don't fix it." Nothing at KPMG appeared to be broken. There were no glaring cultural issues that needed to be addressed. Indeed, waiting till something goes wrong before doing anything about it is definitely a choice a lot of employers make. Such employers keep my consulting practice busy. In contrast, I've never had a call from KPMG. In fact, I called KPMG executives to ask if I could include the company in my book.

KPMG, I was told, began by conducting research into its work environment. Researchers gathered information from employees at all levels and administered an employee survey focused on three issues: inclusivity, tolerance and advancement. The survey revealed that there were differences in the way employees responded, depending on gender and ethnicity.

An employee survey is always a good place to start. It can give a sense of what is going on in the workplace. But then there's the issue of how to interpret a survey. KPMG used the results as a platform for conversations with employees.

From these conversations, KPMG learned that although women and members of visible minorities were getting hired and promoted, these individuals frequently encountered "micro-inequities" during the course of their employment: environments that spawned subtle disadvantages for them. The micro-inequalities, which had not previously registered on KPMG's radar, were the result of inaccurate assumptions, beliefs about differences that influenced people's behaviour toward one another. For instance, say a manager has tickets to a sporting event to give away. The manager assumes the women wouldn't want to go, and gives the tickets away instead to the men. Or say someone organizing employee events assumes alcohol should always be served, or makes assumptions as to how working parents need to be supported.

While there was no overt prejudice at KPMG, the survey revealed that people's assumptions affected perceptions and, in some cases, resulted in the perpetuation of stereotypes. The company wanted to raise awareness about these perceptions and stereotypes. KPMG initiated leadership roundtable discussions called "Dead Moose on the Table" to initiate conversations about common misperceptions and myths affecting decision making. Leaders were forced to look hard at themselves and at the assumptions they made about their staff. "Do we think about the fact that some of the people we work with may not be able to work on a Friday night, or may not be able to eat at the group restaurant? How many assume a working mother does not want that plum out-of-town assignment or is unable to do the overtime on a key engagement? Do you assume that the working moms on your team are less committed?"

Self-assessment and open discussions of difficult issues have become a core component of KPMG's culture strategy. All employees, particularly leaders, are reminded to constantly monitor and assess themselves, to ensure that they are not operating on ingrained assumptions. At every level, employees participate in conversations aimed at raising awareness about assumptions and attitudes that may be affecting workplace relationships.

Does this strategy sound good to you? Well, please don't jump up, call a team meeting and force everyone to look at the "dead moose" on the table. Employees can't acknowledge the moose until you've established the right conditions.

Let's recap what KPMG did. The firm knew it wanted to be an Employer of Choice. To realize that goal, executives decided to formalize their commitment to a respectful, diverse and inclusive culture. They were determined to live up to the mission and values statements they already had, to infuse them into their corporate culture. They decided that the first order of business was to talk about diversity. According to Val Duffey, HR director of communications and governance at KPMG, the purpose of this strategy was "to let everyone know that this is the kind of workplace we are, and we do not tolerate any behaviour that is not in accordance with our values. If people were not on side, there was now nowhere to hide."

The next step was to design and conduct the survey. When its results were in, KPMG chose to spend a full year holding conversations at the top of the house with key leaders and management, so that they understood what the survey meant. Only when all senior management had scrutinized themselves and their own behaviour, when everyone at the top was truly on board, did executives broaden the discussion to include the next level of leadership.

KPMG made another purposeful choice: to set up its diversity initiative as a business strategy led by a senior partner. The human resources department was charged with supporting "local champions." Decision makers at local offices are accountable for developing and implementing their own diversity action plans to support and foster a respectful workplace culture aligned with the corporate vision and values.

We are all familiar with the principle "lead by example." Unfortunately, many workers across Canada do not see this principle in action. KPMG, Four Seasons and other Employers of Choice embrace this principle on a daily basis. While maintaining a respectful workplace culture is a responsibility that must be recognized and shared by everyone in an organization, such a culture cannot exist without a 100 percent commitment from those at the top. Leaders must be prepared to admit to biases and problematic behaviours, fallibility, imperfection and being human. They have to be open to feedback. Only when we respect ourselves and are truly willing to examine and acknowledge our own behaviours can we choose to change those behaviours.

That day I stood up in my session and owned up to my prejudices, I laid the foundation for a dialogue with the attendees about theirs. Although I maintained my position of power as course leader and subject expert, I had taken action to equalize the power imbalance. In admitting my own behavioural shortcomings, I created a connection based on our shared humanity. In exposing my own unflattering behaviour, I gave them permission to talk about theirs.

Easy for me, though. I am not working in a hierarchical organization with legacies of command and control culture. I don't have to be concerned about being macho. I can admit to eating quiche. For some of you, sticking hot pokers into your eyes may seem more appealing than talking about your prejudices and assumptions with co-workers.

But as Abraham Maslow said, "Life is about growth. You can either go back to your comfort zone or you must be willing to go forward and face your fears again and again." If you want to build a respectful workplace culture, if you want to be an Employer of Choice, you have to be prepared to take off the rose-coloured glasses. You must see yourself and your workplace as they truly are. You need to be willing to participate in difficult discussions about your own biases and assumptions, and be willing to admit to them, sometimes publicly. A good place to start is with your beliefs about leadership and power. Ask yourself what you think a good leader looks like. What assumptions do you have about "strengths and weaknesses" relative to leadership in the workplace?

A respectful workplace culture is not about zero tolerance. It is not about good guys and bad guys. It is not fear based. The Road to Respect is paved with courage, honesty, trust, dialogue, support, patience, tolerance, strength and forgiveness. And we need to travel down that road slowly, leading by example, taking small steps and celebrating every milestone along the way.

Part 2

Respect – A Core Value
in a Values-Based Culture

4

A Values-Based Culture

Our Ten Operating Values Remain the Foundation of Our Actions and Decisions. Living by these values creates the type of environment we all desire: an environment in which we exceed the expectations of our customers and those of each other, where we don't just satisfy people, we wow them.

—INTUIT, INC.

ONE EVENING IN the early 1980s, after a long day of work, Scott Cook and his wife, Signe Ostiby, were in their kitchen organizing and paying their bills. As Cook listened to his wife complain about the time-consuming task, he had an idea. Everyone was getting a personal computer these days. What if he could develop a computer program that would help people pay their bills and manage their finances more efficiently?

Like Issy Sharp, Cook was a man of action. In 1983, he founded Intuit, a company that created software to help people manage their finances. Initially, it was just Cook and Ostiby developing, wrapping and shipping their new software from their kitchen. Cook, however, had bigger plans. As he worked, he thought about the kind of company he wanted to build. He developed a clear vision that would guide him as his business developed. He made a conscious decision to build a values-based company committed to integrity and fair play.

As we have already discussed, the key to a values-based company is not the values posted on its boardroom walls. It is about translating the values into behaviours employees experience in every aspect of their working lives. It is about using those values to guide business decisions about every business practice. And that is what distinguishes Four Seasons Corporation, Intuit and the other Employers of Choice from scores of other companies. Cook made sure that the values he felt passionate about, the values he knew were critical to creating the workplace culture he envisaged, remained relevant and ever-present as his organization grew and experienced cultural change.

By 1993, Cook and Ostiby were no longer working in their kitchen. Intuit now employed 500 and Cook worried about the effect of rapid growth on his vision of a values-based company. He understood the importance of having everyone, regardless of the company's size, on board and living Intuit's corporate values. A critical step in that process, he realized, was to ensure that all staff would relate to, understand and experience those corporate values.

At that point in his company's history, as a man of action with a clear vision of success, Cook made a choice. He shut down his company for a day, took all 500 employees off site, divided them into teams and gave each team some butcher paper. Their task? To brainstorm and capture ideas that would be used to develop Intuit's vision, mission and operating values.

Cook certainly could have made another choice. He could have elaborated on his own ideas, or sat down with his senior managers and gotten their input. Alternatively, with business booming, he could have hired consultants to develop a "vision and values" product for him. However, concerned with integrity and fair play, Cook chose to clearly demonstrate to all his employees that he was living his values. He chose to lead by example. He shrugged off the easiest, quickest, cheapest path and opted for the respectful path.

When I am delivering Respectful Workplace Training, I am interested in provoking dialogue between co-workers about respectful behaviours in their workplace. While Canadian Human Rights law defines respectful behaviour as non-discriminatory, there are scores of other behaviours that employees – particularly in a diverse, multicultural workplace – consider to be disrespectful. As we've already established, talking about those varying perspectives is key to eliminating disrespectful actions.

Regardless of an employee group's composition, there are two behaviours universally defined as respectful. Someone in every session refers to the first of these, the Golden Rule. The other is inclusion and consultation. Most of us believe that if I am in a position of power and have to make a decision that affects you, I am behaving respectfully when I consider you in my decision making. I need to show you in a concrete fashion that you are valued as an individual, and that your opinion counts.

When Cook made a decision to close down his company for a day to get his employees' input on company values, he sent a very clear, respectful message to his employees. He demonstrated his personal philosophy about organizational power, integrity and fair play. That inclusive process produced Intuit's ten operating values, which have remained virtually unchanged since.

At Intuit, like at the Four Seasons, the ten operating values are more than a paper strategy. They define and shape the corporate culture and work experience of each employee. Everyone who works at Intuit embraces them. While Intuit's distinctive values reflect the nature of their business, they have something in common with those of the Four Seasons, KPMG and the other Employers of Choice. That commonality is – you guessed it – the inclusion of respect as a core value in their corporate culture.

The day after I heard Beth Wilson from KPMG speak, I set about finding other Employers of Choice. I looked at the "Best Companies to Work For" lists, then researched each company to determine whether they had a respectful, inclusive culture. Intuit popped up everywhere: in *Report on Business*, Best Places to Work 2007, Great Places to Work, Fortune 100 and the Mediacorp Canada lists, among others. My research showed that, consistent with other Employers of Choice, Intuit had a values-based culture that embraced respect as a core value. Intuit doesn't call it a "Golden Rule culture" as Four Seasons does, but the description of how respect fits in to Intuit's corporate culture is similar: "We treat each other, our business partners and our shareholders with the same care and respect with which we treat our customers."

Here are questions I posed to all the Employers of Choice I chose to interview for this book: How do you translate the core value of respect so that it is the experience of employees in the workplace? How do you make employees feel respected and included? What does respectful communication look like? What does respectful supervision look like?

I wasn't looking for theoretical answers. I know the theory. I articulated that when I launched my website: "The focus of my practice is in assisting my clients to establish and maintain a workplace that promotes respectful behaviours and inclusive practices, a workplace where each individual employee feels valued and is motivated to be productive at work."

Employers of Choice have developed a business model that flows from their core value of respect. How do you live the Golden Rule in business? "People, product, profit…in that order. That is our business model," says Ellen du Bellay, vice president of learning and development at Four Seasons Hotels. "Our philosophy is that if we treat people right, they will deliver the product and profit will follow."

Intuit's ten core values are the glue that holds everything together. The firm regards values as the most important aspect of its business. "You start from that and solve from there. That goes for everyone throughout the entire organization," says Jane Sillberg, director of human resources for Intuit Canada. At values-based cultures, the values are the framework from which every business decision and practice flows.

I celebrate the choices that Employers of Choice make in building their businesses. In my mind, they are our modern day heroes. They make a choice to promote the notion, enshrined in the universal declaration of human rights, that all of us, as members of the human race, are deserving of respectful and dignified treatment. They choose to use their power to create values-based workplace cultures that promote respectful, empowering and inclusive practices. In upcoming chapters, we will look at some of those practices. As we have already learned, the Road to Respect will not be without challenges. However, as author Frank A. Clark put it, "If you can find a path with no obstacles, it probably doesn't lead anywhere."

5

Values-Based Hiring –
Respectful Recruitment

Well, first of all, it starts with hiring. We are zealous about hiring. If you start with the type of person you want to hire, presumably you can build a workforce that is prepared for the culture you desire.

—HERB KELLEHER, CEO of Southwest Airlines

A NUMBER OF years ago, I was helping a client deal with a member of his executive team who was acting out of synch with the firm's family-based corporate culture. My client had been taken by surprise when employees complained about sexual harassment and bullying in relation to this executive. Less than a year earlier, my client had met this executive at a conference, gone for a drink and hit it off with him. As luck would have it, this individual was looking to make a career move and my client was in the market for someone with his skill set. They had a great time getting to know each other. As for reference checks, "Who needs them?" my client explained, "When you have a gut feel about someone."

While I am all for trusting one's intuition, gut feel is not quite enough to ensure you get the right person for the job. My client learned this the hard way. And, as my client also learned, steps missed at the recruitment stage can mean unanticipated costs. It takes time and money to solve problems created by recruitment blunders. Unfortunately, I've seen many organizations fail to ask the questions that ensure an effective and respectful recruitment process.

This is definitely not the case with Employers of Choice, which recognize the importance of recruitment as a critical component of their success. The third value on Intuit's list is "It's the People," and the fourth is "Seek the Best." Recruitment is key to both. The company spends a lot of time and effort finding the right person for every job. This means hiring someone who shares company values and will fit in with the corporate culture. There is no compromising on that position. When recruiting for a recent vacancy in human resources, the Intuit recruiter screened eighty-two candidates before presenting anyone to the selection committee.

At Intuit, a candidate who gets past the screening stage under-goes a number of panel interviews, up to ten for senior positions. While panel members vary with the position being filled, they always involve people who will work with the new hire.

This is not lip service. It is a genuine, consultative system that involves all the stakeholders. The recruitment process is open, fair, consistent and inclusive. Everyone's feedback is solicited and con-sidered. Prospective candidates, meanwhile, get a clear message about the type of culture in which they will be working. They get a firsthand look at a team-based, consultative, respectful culture. The goal is a good fit. It is not just about skills. It is about skills, behaviours and shared values.

The same goes for internal selection. Intuit actively promotes from within; most of its leaders come from the ranks. According to Beverly Kaye and Sharon Jordan-Evans, authors of *Love 'Em or*

Lose 'Em, "The front-line manager is the most important element in attracting and retaining employees."[1] My own experience certainly confirms their research. Managers are typically hired for their technical, not people skills. As a result, we often end up with managers who can manage products but not people. Ironically, the people portion of the equation is what management is all about. The failure to hire and promote managers and supervisors with critical people skills is a costly blunder for any business.

Intuit recognizes the importance of employee/supervisor relationships. Managers are selected for their people skills. This emphasis flows directly from their third and sixth stated values: "It's the People" and "Speak, Respond and Listen." At Intuit, "...technical people are promoted, however, we are careful not to take people who are just technical. We look for the base of people skills. We look for people that live the values," says Jane Sillberg, director of human resources for Intuit Canada. In order to determine if that candidate is living Intuit's values, the internal selection involves all the stakeholders. This is consistent with external recruitment. The selection process includes asking questions and measuring competencies directly related to Intuit's leadership philosophy. And that philosophy, which flows from the firm's values, is all about supporting and empowering the people one is leading.

So how does this recruitment and selection process demonstrate respect as a core value? Let's think about the message you get as an employee working on a team looking for a new member or leader. Rather than wait with bated breath to see who you will be working with, you are involved in the process. Rather than gossiping with your co-workers at the water cooler, and trading any details you may have overheard, you all share information openly. You have been included in communication at every stage of the process. You and your co-workers may even be on one of the interview panels. If that is the case, you are supported and coached by your business unit's human resources partner to prepare you for it. After the panel, you are included in the debrief. You get to share your thoughts, which will be considered by others involved in the process. You are not ignored, discounted or ridiculed. You are a participant in the decision-making process.

The message you get is fundamentally a respectful one. It says that you count. You are part of the process. You are a valued member of the team and have a say in the issues that affect you at work. And you believe this message not because you hear it or see it written down somewhere. You believe it because you experience it and you live it at work. You are empowered to be an active participant in creating your own work environment. You feel respected as a person and as an employee.

Now let's look at it from the perspective of the new hire. What message does that individual get about respect as a core value? The consultative and inclusive interview process means she/he is joining a team that is open and welcoming rather than resentful, unhappy, fearful or hostile. His or her co-workers are looking forward to working with their new team member.

Here's a different story from a company that has never made Employer of Choice. Rumours were flying about a person from another location being transferred into "Judy's" department. No one knew the employee personally. Gossip was that this woman got the job because of who she knew in the upper echelons of the organization. Even though this information was unconfirmed, team members felt angry. It meant local employees who seemed perfect for the job had been bypassed. The week before the new employee was scheduled to start, the team leader called a meeting and formally announced that this woman would be joining their team. It wasn't long before everyone was questioning their new team member's qualifications. According to "Judy," the comments were blatantly disrespectful and mean-spirited. She felt uncomfortable with what she was hearing, but was not sure what to do. She was particularly concerned that her manager was listening to and participating in the barrage of negativity.

The process I have just outlined was neither fair nor respectful, yet in my experience, it's the rule rather than the exception. The inevitable result is lowered morale and a potentially hostile environment for the new employee. The new staff member becomes targeted as the problem, although in reality she is as much a victim of an unfair process as her new teammates.

Values-based hiring is a key component to ensuring that an organization is living its values. Four Seasons "hires for attitude, then trains for skill. We are always looking for a person that is nice." When I heard that from Ellen du Bellay, vice president of learning and development at Four Seasons Corporation, I paused. They hire people just because they are nice?

Although Intuit and Four Seasons are in very different industries, their recruiting processes are strikingly similar. At Four Seasons, like at Intuit, every applicant can expect to go through a series of hiring interviews. The minimum number of interviews for any new employee, including maids and kitchen staff, is five. Each prospective employee will go through a screening interview, a departmental interview and a divisional interview. If they make it though those three, they will be interviewed by the hotel manger. The last step, known as "the Golden Rule interview," is with the hotel's general manager. The purpose of this last interview is to ensure that new employees truly fit the corporate culture.

Once they make it in, Four Season's employees tend to stick around. Many move up through the ranks. The average tenure of the management committee is twenty-two years. This occurs by design. The corporation wants individuals to pursue a career at Four Seasons. "If we've done everything right, our new hire will be a lifelong employee. Our annual turnover is seventeen percent compared to an industry average of thirty-six percent, and we believe our culture is creating this result," says du Bellay.

The company actively promotes from within and rarely hires management from outside. From experience, executives know that outside hires at the managerial level often fail. The reason? They just don't fit in with the Golden Rule culture. One general manager who was an outside hire decided to save money by laying off some housekeepers when his hotel lost business due to a depressed local economy. In the end, it was the general manager who was laid off –

while all the housekeepers stayed put. He wasn't working within the firm's business model. In a Golden Rule culture it is "people, product, profit – in that order, under every circumstance."

I heard the same theme expressed when I spoke with Cliff Yeo, human resources advisor with Canada Safeway. "Virtually 100 percent of our management has come up through the ranks. Maybe four have not. That is a purposeful choice. There is more knowledge of our Safeway culture. The few that we tried from outside, it just wasn't what we would call successful. We have really good people who work for us. There is no need to go outside. I would say the best people in retail work for us."

Recruitment and internal selection can look quite different in organizations that do not embrace respect as a core value. Employees at one organization told me, "A game we like to play around here when a job is posted is to read the job description and figure out who they want to get it. We can pretty much figure out who it is they want, because the job description is completely tailored to skills or educational qualifications that only that one person has. Sometimes they post the job, and then if they don't get the person they want, they just take it down and change the qualifications so that the person they want will apply. Or if they don't want anyone internal to get it, all of a sudden this job requires skills that no one around here has."

Another company: "We have no idea how people get jobs around here. I mean, we know how it is supposed to work, but then all of a sudden this person gets the job and you are just left shaking your head. Around here, it is all about who you know." Or, "The way it is around here, the worse you perform, the more likely you are to get promoted. They just take the problem and shift it to another department."

Then there's blatant favouritism. The manager's favourite gets the plum assignment or promotion regardless of skill. In many cases, the bully keeps getting promoted. I have had employees tell me they applied for promotion and are told that they didn't get it because they were needed in their current position – implying that their current competence precludes any career development. I've also encountered cases where co-workers believe that an individual got a job because he or she is a member of a traditionally disadvantaged group. The perception is that the employer wants to be seen as politically correct.

As a consultant, I hear these stories from the employees of my clients, but I don't always have a way of knowing what is actually going on. Bottom line, though, is that the recruitment and selection process is being handled in a less than open, inclusive way, and that gets employees complaining about perceived unfair treatment. They're describing processes that make them feel they are neither respected nor valued. Even if they're misinterpreting matters, the end result is the same, an angry and frustrated rather than engaged, focused and motivated workforce.

Often things go off the rails due to a failure to communicate. In some cases the process is a fair one, and the employees' perception is incorrect. Without clearly communicated and deliberate information sharing, employees are left to come up with their own conclusions about why things happen the way they do. I encounter this over and over in my work. No one means to be disrespectful, but in our fast-paced contemporary workplaces, effective communication gets overlooked. Inevitably, employees feel out of the loop, disconnected from the organization and its purpose.

In a values-based workplace culture, that outcome simply cannot occur. Such firms do not compromise on commitment to the core values. As we have already established, in a respectful workplace culture, respect is a core value. This means that every practice is evaluated from the perspective of respect. "Is the way we are doing this respectful or not?" That question must be asked at every stage and for every process.

Intuit, Four Seasons and other Employers of Choice make deliberate decisions to design recruitment and selection processes that flow from and reflect their core values, values that embody the principle of respect. That is the key to the success of these practices and businesses. Remember, this is not about cookie-cutter culture.

It's easy to attempt to copy or transpose their processes, but these organizations' recruitment process may not fit your organization. Creating a respectful culture is about designing processes that will work in your company, for your business, based on your values. The commonality must be the inclusion of respect as the foundation of all of your business practices. To become an Employer of Choice, you need to design a respectful recruitment process that works for your organization and ensures that you hire individuals who are a good fit with your desired corporate culture.

6

Can We Talk?
Power, Fear and Disrespectful
Behaviours in the Workplace

Contrary to what some people might think, being in a position of power,
whether it is within a business, family, community group or any other
organization, does not give any person the right to berate, belittle, intim-
idate or ridicule another human being.

—PETER LEGGE, speaker, author, businessman

BEFORE YOU CAN map out your road to a respectful workplace
culture, you have to determine the starting point for your journey. It is difficult to move forward if you don't know where you
are. In order to determine your starting point, you need to assess
your current corporate culture. Both KPMG and Intuit started their
journey with information gathering and employee involvement –

absolutely the best way to go. Aim to uncover relevant information that demonstrates your core value of respect. Solicit, include, respect and act on employees' opinions.

If employees are resistant, reluctant or downright afraid to express their opinions – even when directly asked to do so – that has to do with the dynamic of power.

You have probably experienced this yourself. You sit in an important meeting, but find the conversation monopolized by others. You offer an opinion that is ignored or dismissed. Someone raises a question on which no one seems willing to express an opinion. That is, until the meeting is over. And then, by the water cooler, in the cafeteria, in the smoking pit or wherever folks congregate to talk, opinions are expressed loudly and discussion ensues. Opinions that seemed accepted in the meeting room are now hotly debated or ridiculed. People who never opened their mouths in the meeting now can't seem to keep them closed. All this says much about the corporate culture and its lack of openness and inclusiveness.

I can tell a lot about organizational culture even before I meet employees in a training session. For instance, when a client and I talk beforehand about how to group employees for the session, and the client wants to group them along hierarchical lines, I know it's a command and control organization. In some cases, the client may insist that a mix of management and employees be present, implying a more progressive structure. Only once have I had a company president and vice president insist on sitting in on a session with front-line employees. We had a lively session that day; employees seemed to feel free to participate and express themselves. Too bad this is very much the exception.

More typically, despite my standard spiel about the importance of a participatory session, the presence of a supervisor or manager causes a cone of silence to descend. Then, participants use their anonymous feedback forms to express true feelings. The comments are direct and to the point: "If you really want to have a participatory session, you need to get those management employees out of the room!"

Very few, if any, organizations say that fear is one of the core values upon which their culture is based. Nonetheless, my experience is that fear is pervasive, influential and directly tied to employee motivation and behaviour. Fear is often created and promoted by disrespectful workplace practices. Whether or not these practices are intentional, in the vast majority of workplaces, employees are afraid to openly express themselves.

This is a problem. If your workplace culture is creating and fostering fear, that makes it very difficult to engage in the type of honest dialogue discussed in Chapter Three. It is very difficult to have a "dead moose on the table" conversation if people are afraid to express themselves. So, one of the first stops on the Road to Respect is to ascertain the level of fear that exists in your workplace, and determine what behaviours or practices are contributing to that fear.

Is There a Bully in Your Workplace?

Bullying is the sexual harassment of twenty years ago; everybody knows about it, but nobody wants to admit it.

— LEWIS MALTBY, president of the U.S. National Workrights
Institute (2001)

Not long after I was hired at the airline, my boss commented that she really liked to work with bright people. That sounded logical to me. I like to work with bright people too. She said she had purposely hired me because she knew I was smart and capable. Then she went on to say that most people don't do so because they feel threatened.

It turns out she was right.

Ruth Namie was a bright and capable woman who had worked as a corporate training director, management consultant and retail manager. Then she decided she wanted to become a clinical psychologist. She earned her PHD and began working in a psychiatric clinic. Unfortunately for her, the woman to whom she was reporting did not share my boss's perspective on supervising smart, capable people. Ruth found herself on the receiving end of negative treatment she had never experienced and couldn't even name. Eventually, with the help of her partner in life, social psychology professor Dr. Gary Namie, she figured it out. It was workplace bullying.

As a consultant, I deal with an increasing number of workplace bullying cases. This is not because more people are being bullied – people have always been bullied at work – but because of a growing awareness of workplace bullying, thanks to people like Dr. Namie and her husband. After Ruth's horrific experiences at the hand of her bully boss, the Namies decided to talk publicly about this destructive behaviour.

We all know the saying, "knowledge is power." The Namies wrote a book entitled *The Bully at Work* and started a consulting practice devoted to spreading the word about workplace bullying. One important outcome of the Namies' work was that they named and defined the behaviour Ruth had experienced. According to the Namies, "Bullying at work is the repeated, malicious, health-endangering mistreatment of one employee (the 'target') by one or more employees (the 'perpetrators'). The mistreatment is psychological violence, a mix of verbal and strategic assaults to prevent the target from performing work well. It is illegitimate conduct in that it prevents work getting done. Thus, an employer's legitimate business interests are not met."[1]

The Namies call workplace bullying "status-blind harassment." By "status" they mean what we in Canada call the prohibited grounds, like race, sex or religion, which are listed in human rights legislation. I agree that there are important similarities between workplace harassment and workplace bullying. Both are fundamentally disrespectful and problems that employers and employees need to understand.

One important distinction involves the dynamic of power as it manifests in bullying complaints, as opposed to harassment complaints. Another crucial difference relates to intention and outcome. In addition, workplace harassment arises as a legal issue through human rights law in Canada, while workplace bullying is for the most part currently not a legal concern for employers in Canada. Let's start there.

Intention vs. Outcome –
Workplace Bullying vs. Discriminatory Harassment

Clients call me on a regular basis to investigate harassments complaints. However, after asking a few simple questions, I often discover that what I am being asked to deal with is, in fact, a complaint of "personal" harassment. Some of you may be familiar with the term personal harassment, as many workplace harassment policies and/ or collective agreements refer to it. Some human rights/harassment policies include sexual harassment, defined as harassment related to gender, and personal harassment, encompassing everything else. I refer to of the latter as a non-limiting definition.

What's the big deal? Harassment is harassment, right? In fact that is not the case. Workplace harassment flows from human rights law in Canada and is very specifically defined. Other behaviour – bullying, conflict and just bad behaviour – is often lumped into a workplace policy as personal harassment.

When I worked at the airline, our policy had this non-limiting definition, which included personal harassment. Harassment was defined as "conduct in the workplace that creates an intimidating, threatening, coercive or hostile work environment." While it echoed the Canadian Human Rights Act, it also included "other activities that intrude upon a person's or group's dignity or that create an intimidating, hostile or offensive atmosphere." These other activities, which can include anything an employee considers offensive, amount to personal harassment.

The problem with this loosely worded definition and the term personal harassment is that it opens the door to a host of complaints not covered legally. When I took over administration of the corporate harassment policy at the airline, I experienced first-hand what happens when we allow every issue to be processed as a harassment complaint. A supervisor tries to talk to an employee about job performance and all of a sudden the employee accuses the supervisor of harassment. A conflict between two co-workers erupts and one decides to charge the other with harassment. We were inundated with complaints we were required to investigate due to that personal harassment language in our policy.

I am not sure how workplaces in Canada came to have the term "personal harassment" in their vocabulary, but if a group ever formed to eradicate the term from our lexicon, I would join! After working with the airline policy for a while, I initiated a union/management harassment policy review. I wanted to adopt a more limited definition of harassment, one that reflected the law and did not include "personal harassment." After reading a decision by British Columbia arbitrator Heather Laing, I had the evidence I needed to support my views before the committee: "Every act by which a person causes some form of anxiety to another could be labelled as harassment. But if this is so, there can be no safe interaction between human beings. Sadly, we are not perfect. All of us, on occasion, are stupid, heedless, thoughtless and insensitive. The question then is, when are we guilty of harassment?

"I do not think that every act of workplace foolishness was intended to be captured by the word 'harassment.' This is a serious word, to be used seriously and applied vigorously when the occasion warrants its use… Not every employment bruise should be treated under this process. It would be unfortunate if the harassment process was used to vent feelings of minor discontent or general unhappiness with life in the workplace, so as to trivialize those cases where substantial workplace abuses have occurred."[2]

My experience at the airline and in my practice reflects what Laing wrote. This harassment label can devastate the individual accused. I have seen scores of cases where the process has been misused and individuals have been unfairly accused. Sadly, regardless of the outcome of the investigation, the label seems to stick. The damage is done when the accusation is made.

The inclusion of the term personal harassment in corporate harassment polices and collective agreements is, in many cases, directly responsible for encouraging disrespectful behaviour in the first place. It encourages labelling, blaming, accusing and victimization. It keeps us from understanding and appreciating the myriad of disrespectful behaviours we encounter in our workplaces. It muddies the water.

While some of the issues processed as personal harassment might constitute harassment as it is defined in a dictionary, the fact is, harassment is a concern in the workplace because the law defines it as a type of discriminatory behaviour. Remember what I said in Chapter Two about the law and obligation for employers to provide a respectful working environment? Canadian human rights laws, which apply in the sphere of employment, define discrimination as disrespectful behaviour.

To ensure we all understand what we are talking about when we refer to discrimination in employment, here is a standard definition. Discrimination refers to unfair, differential treatment of individuals or groups and is prohibited by law. It may be intentional or unintentional and can result in one individual or group having an advantage over another, or cause an individual or group to be excluded from activities which they have the right to be included in.

Notice that discrimination is illegal and unfair treatment. Notice, too, that "discrimination may be intentional or unintentional." The law does not care whether or not someone meant to discriminate. The law is concerned only with outcome, which means "equality" in the workplace.

In Canadian law, equality does not mean we are all exactly the same and therefore equal. The equality with which it is concerned is equality of opportunity and outcome. In theory, we should all be "equally" able to take advantage of work-related opportunities and have access to work-related outcomes. When discrimination occurs, an individual is being disadvantaged relative to others at work. An individual discriminated against might not get a job, a promotion, or receive the same salary as other employees.

In order to prove discrimination, the individual must demonstrate that he or she is not experiencing equality of outcome because of race, sex, ethnicity, sexual orientation or some other category listed in the relevant human rights legislation. By "human rights legislation," I am referring to whether or not a company is federally regulated – in which case it would fall under the Canadian Human Rights Act – or provincially regulated, in which case it would fall under provincial human rights legislation. Each piece of legislation is different, and variations exist in the personal characteristics included.

One of my hot tips in Chapter Two concerned statutory liability, which means employers must deal with complaints of discrimination when they occur in the workplace. Statutory liability was imposed because of the traditional power imbalance between employers and employees.

Workplace harassment, which I refer to as discriminatory harassment, is a concern for us at work because it flows directly from the issue of discrimination. Discriminatory harassment is very different from the dictionary's definition of harassment. It is defined as a type of discrimination and means engaging in a course of annoying comments or conduct that is known or ought reasonably to be known to be unwelcome, that is tied to a prohibited ground of discrimination and that detrimentally affects the work environment or leads to adverse job-related consequences for the victim of harassment.

The same issues of intention and outcome apply. We don't consider the element of intention. We don't care if someone meant to harass someone. That said, if we can show that the behaviour was in fact intentional, we may be able to argue for greater damages for pain and suffering. However, the bottom line is, intention does not have to be proven to substantiate a complaint of discriminatory harassment.

Whenever I write policies for clients, I use the term "discriminatory harassment." My goal is to distinguish this behaviour from other behaviours captured by the misnomer of personal harassment.

One of the behaviours traditionally captured under the personal harassment umbrella is workplace bullying. To appreciate the differences between discriminatory harassment and workplace bullying – both disrespectful behaviours – let's take another look at the definition of workplace bullying and compare it to the definition of discriminatory harassment. Here again is the Namies' definition: "Bullying at work is the repeated, malicious, health-endangering mistreatment of one employee (the target) by one or more employees (the perpetrator). The mistreatment is psychological violence, a mix of verbal and strategic assaults to prevent the target from performing work well. It is illegitimate conduct in that it prevents work getting done. Thus, an employer's legitimate business interests are not met."

Another definition of workplace bullying comes from the Canadian Centre for Occupational Health and Safety: "Bullying is usually seen as acts or verbal comments that could 'mentally' hurt or isolate a person in the workplace. Sometimes, bullying can involve negative physical contact as well. Bullying usually involves repeated incidents or a pattern of behaviour that is intended to intimidate, offend, degrade or humiliate a particular person or group of people. It has also been described as the assertion of power through aggression."

Whereas our definition of discrimination says "whether intentional or unintentional," bulling here is defined as "malicious... behaviour that is intended to intimidate." Workplace bullying is considered intentional; an individual makes a choice to engage in bullying behaviour. When we are dealing with a complaint of workplace bullying, we must be able to show that the behaviour was intentional and purposeful.

When we look at the outcome of bullying complaints, we are looking for "health endangering," "psychological assault" and "acts or comments that could mentally hurt." Workplace bullying is not about equality of outcome. An individual being bullied at work does not need to show disadvantage relative to others due to race, gender or ethnicity. While workplace bullying often disadvantages the individual being bullied, the usual outcome (and one that must be proven in bullying complaints) is harm. Bullying results in physical, psychological or emotional harm due to the intentional behaviour of someone else in the workplace. Usually, in workplace bullying, that someone else is someone in a position of power – "the assertion of power through aggression."

The Namies did more than define the mistreatment Ruth experienced. They also conducted a large research study on the phenomenon of workplace bullying. One interesting finding was that while men and women are equally likely to be bullies, women tend to be victimized in the vast majority of cases. They found that in many instances, the "targets" of workplace bullying are bright, competent women and men who are good at their jobs, as was Ruth Namie.

This is another factor that distinguishes workplace bullying from discriminatory harassment. Human rights law was structured in response to the historical discrimination in our society. Some individuals experience discriminatory behaviour as a fact of life. They are "targeted" for their race, ethnicity, gender or sexual orientation. Unfortunately, because they may be victimized in an array of situations beyond the workplace, they often come to expect discriminatory behaviour, and learn to cope with the experience. They may have support systems within their communities and families, many of whom are empathetic due to their own experiences with discrimination.

Targets of workplace bullying, on the other hand, have typically never experienced the type of behaviour they encounter at the hands of their bully. As the Namies' research documented, individuals targeted in the workplace are generally not the "outcasts and social misfits" we associate with the victims of schoolyard bullying. Workplace bullying happens to people who are intelligent, capable, articulate and well liked, individuals whose previous life experience has left them completely unprepared for being targeted.

This adds to the health-endangering outcome of workplace bullying. Individuals are initially so taken aback that they tend to dismiss it, try harder or look at ways they can influence the situation. Typically empathetic individuals concerned with fair play and just behaviour, these targets generally don't react quickly and often try to reason with the bully – only making things worse. The perpetrator's bullying behaviours are often so subtle that it takes a long time for a pattern to become evident. By then the target is usually seriously affected, both mentally and physically. Research shows that one-third to one-half of stress-related illnesses reported in Great Britain are due to workplace bullying.[3]

Those who discriminate at work may be bosses or a co-worker. This is not the case in workplace bullying. The Namies' research confirms that in more than seventy-five percent of cases, the bully holds the power – just as in Ruth's experience of the bully boss. While my own experience supports this research, I have also seen numerous examples of peer to peer bullying. Then the bully relies on some other source of power: knowledge, seniority, persona and/or workplace connections to intimidate the target. Power and workplace bullying are intricately linked.

Bullying behaviour and human history are also linked. Bullying is about power and control. As we learned in Chapter Two, bullying behaviour was purposely employed in militaristic, male-dominated command and control workplace cultures and formed the foundational cultural model of many workplaces up until quite recently. Unfortunately for women like Ruth Namie, the remnants of that legacy still flourish in contemporary workplaces.

It is this legacy that has encouraged workplace cultures that promote win/lose, us-and-them competitiveness and the desire to dominate. Organizations with traditional power-based structures are ideal environments for fostering bullying behaviour, and sometimes even encourage individuals who might not otherwise engage in bullying behaviour to do so.

Bullying is like bacteria. It needs the right environment in which to thrive. In business, that environment is a disrespectful workplace culture.

A Culture of Bullying

Helen Green was a bright, capable woman. She had a high-profile job at Deutsche Bank AG in London. In 2006, Green gained notoriety as a victim of workplace bullying. What caught the attention of media and employers everywhere was the $1.7 million (Cdn) settlement she was awarded.

Green, who worked in the firm's secretarial division, claimed that she suffered psychiatric injury because of "offensive, abusive, intimidating, denigrating, bullying, humiliating, patronizing, infantile and insulting words and behaviour." She claimed that Deutsche Bank knew about the bullying, particularly after her nervous breakdown, but did nothing to stop it. The High Court described the treatment Green received as "...domineering, disrespectful, dismissive, confrontational and designed to undermine and belittle her in the view of others" and found that she was working in "a culture of bullying."[4]

A culture of bullying. How did they come to that conclusion? Well, here's one factor that influenced that finding: when Green told her direct supervisor what was happening to her, he told her that bullying was just a fact of life one had to accept. He himself had been bullied at boarding school and was treated "brutally" by the hierarchy at the bank. Bullying was part of the workplace culture. It was "the way it is around here."

According to the Namies, workplace bullying is two to three times more common than discriminatory harassment and one in four workers is bullied at work. In 2008 a U.S. research study found that seven out of ten workers are affected.[5]

Despite the lack of formal research on the topic in Canada, a magazine story provided clear evidence that the practice is pervasive here. In December 2006, *BCBusiness* magazine ran a piece on workplace bullying entitled "Bad Boss, Bad Boss." A majority of the magazine's readers reported that they could relate to the topic. In fact, the magazine received such an overwhelming response to the story that the editors ran two subsequent articles on workplace bullying, an April 2007 article, "Battling the Bully," and another in June 2007, "Mob Mentality." Readers learned that bullying behaviour "thrives in tumultuous organizations where bad bosses and sadistic employees are protected by apathetic management or watertight collective agreements, a climate in which good people are afraid to speak out for fear they will also be targeted. Unfortunately, this collective silence condones and even exacerbates the bullying; without a dissenting voice, perpetrators become even more emboldened... Far too many companies still tolerate and even reward bullying bosses."[6]

Why would companies want to tolerate and reward bullying bosses? I've asked myself this question repeatedly, given that I encounter this phenomenon regularly. I believe it boils down to a perceived link between managerial bullying and superior organizational performance.

Remember the young woman from Chapter One, the employer who was well aware of the manager's problematic behaviour? (She had a history of "personal" harassment complaints filed against her.) My client, a senior executive, shared this errant manager's history with me openly during our first meeting. He used what I refer to as the "yes but" perspective. "Yes, she has this history, but she is good at her job. She produces results."

And what was the bullying manager's perspective on the complaints filed against her? She characterized them as "stupid and ridiculous." To her mind, she was a model supervisor who had bent over backward to accommodate a problem employee.

Should we be surprised by this woman's perspective? I think not. Why would she have any reason to think otherwise? Despite the history of complaints against her, the employer had recently promoted her. Regardless of recent discussion about her behaviour, she was never put on notice that it was problematic or had to change. The clear, visible message from executives to the manager was that she was a doing a good job. The equally loud and clear message to the employees was that it was pointless to complain about this woman's behaviour because senior management supported her.

During the interview process, employees told me they had moved departments because of her and would not transfer back while she was there. Employees were crying during interviews with me; many wanted to find other work. A few expressed real concern that the young woman who had launched the latest complaint would leave the organization, leaving others vulnerable as replacement targets. Employees described the atmosphere in which they were accustomed to working as dominated by fear.

Fear can be an incredibly effective motivator in the short term. Management by intimidation often produces results. That is one reason employers continue to reward bullying mangers. Targets of managerial bullying, Ruth Namie among them, consistently try to work harder, better, more efficiently in order to please their bully bosses. Employees working with that bully boss told me how hard everyone was working in an attempt not to "set her off." They made sure to cross every "t" and dot every "i" in hopes they would not give their bully boss an excuse to publicly rebuke or humiliate them.

The young woman who filed the complaint was no exception. Over the three years she'd been bullied, she'd worked herself to the bone to try and please her manager. She was an intelligent, well-liked, capable and hard-working employee who had been moving up in the organization due to her stellar performance. Like Ruth Namie and Helen Green, she had not previously encountered bullying, so it took her a long time to figure out she was not the problem. By that time, her health had deteriorated; she was emotionally exhausted and stressed. She felt defeated. In the end, she quit her job and moved on.

The bully manager, on the other hand, stayed with the organization and no doubt continues to behave as she always has. I made numerous recommendations to the organization, including adopting an anti-bullying policy, but I was not hired to assist in implementing any of them. Why bother? they must have figured. The problem employee (the complainant) was now gone, and the manager would continue to deliver the results they were after.

I learned about the relationship between fear and profitability very early on in my consulting career. I was contracted to diagnose what was causing ongoing employee unrest in a satellite office of a large organization. Arriving in a small town after a long travel day, I was greeted warmly by the branch manager, who insisted on taking me out to dinner. He was a very personable and charming man who had managed the office for years. He told me that the company regularly praised his office's superior sales record, as well as his managerial work. He believed the employees were whining about insignificant issues. Back in my hotel room that night, I wondered warily why the employees were unhappy when their manager seemed such a great guy, and things were going so well. Clearly there was another side to the story.

Although this was before the term "workplace bullying" had gone mainstream, many an employee I spoke with the next day seemed familiar with the behaviour. All this firm's employees were females who'd worked in the office a number of years. When I asked them what the issue was, their reply was unanimous and brief. They looked at each other, looked at me and identified the manager by name. I heard story after story. He ruled by intimidation. He was nasty, arrogant, sneaky and underhanded. He had no respect for staff, referring to them as his lackeys and treating them like children.

It had taken them a while to figure out what was going on. He could be charming, particularly when he wanted something. But he was unpredictable. His technique was to play one employee off against another, to encourage conflict. One day, he treated one employee as the favourite and the next day, someone else. Initially, no one talked about what was going on. But given that it was a small town, employees eventually heard "he said/she said" stories at the local pub. Slowly, they started sharing experiences, including inappropriate sexual comments, insults and even incidents of physical abuse.

When the employees tried to stand up to him collectively, his behaviour grew so volatile they feared being targeted. Amidst all this, they'd all been working extra hard in an effort to avoid being picked on.

Of course, the stress of working in that fearful environment had taken its toll; two employees had taken stress leave, thereby adding to remaining staff's workload. Many of the employees were suffering from physical and emotional complaints they attributed to their jobs. All told me they felt unsafe, oppressed, defeated and trapped.

Quitting wasn't an option; it was a small town with few opportunities for women. Theirs were coveted, well-paid jobs, filled quickly when someone left despite the company's reputation. They needed the income their jobs provided. They couldn't quit!

Neither were they optimistic that I would be able to do anything to improve things for them. A couple of years earlier, they told me, they had dared to get together and write the company's CEO, who had sent a company representative to meet with them and the manager. Not only had this changed nothing; things had gotten worse. The company, they assured me, knew exactly what was going on. They'd contacted human resources staff more than once.

On the flight home, I pondered over what I had heard. The company already knew about the bullying problem but was not taking any action. The next day, when speaking to my contact in human resources, I found out why. In truth, she confided, everybody in her department knew about this manager and his bad behaviour. It had been going on for years. Some staff wanted this manager dealt with, but others protected him because of the consistently high sales of his department.

I worked diligently on my written report and outlined the employer's potential human rights liability. I stressed the toll that the manager's disrespectful behaviour was having, in terms of lost time and productivity. I cited the extent of the demoralized workforce and explained the lack of trust that existed as a result of no action having been taken during previous processes. I made a clear case showing how workplace bullying was bleeding away company profit.

My contact in human resources was impressed with the thoroughness of the report and anticipated it would have the desired impact upon the organizational decision makers. We discussed when I could meet with the senior team to elaborate on my findings and recommendations.

Some time after submitting my report, I followed up. My contact told me that senior management had reviewed the report but had not made any decisions yet. They would not meet with me. Nothing had changed. This organization, while not outwardly stating that they condoned bullying, was in fact aware of, tolerating and rewarding a bullying manager. Clearly, nothing would change until opinion shifted amongst the power brokers at headquarters.

Happily, I succeed more often than not in such efforts, but as a dedicated professional, I can never fully shrug off cases like this. I sometimes picture those women, still working under abominable conditions, still waiting for the letter or complaint that will finally set in motion some measures that make their work lives more tolerable.

Like altogether too many workplaces, this was a legacy of command and control that supported the perceived link between aggressive management tactics and superior business results.

The pervasiveness of this belief really hit me when I was flipping channels on TV one day and stopped on one of my personal favourites – the Food Network. I saw a chef cursing and screaming at his staff, all of whom seemed to be scurrying around in a state of fear and anxiety. "Yes chef," "No chef," they would mumble as he berated them for the allegedly sub-standard dishes they had prepared. He hurled insults and curses as he smashed their creations – food, plates and all. He asked one female chef if she was a dumb blonde and then called her a f__ing Barbie. I saw both female and male staff crying. I was intrigued and horrified at the same time.

It turned out I was watching *Hell's Kitchen*, an appropriately named cooking show starring bully chef Gordon Ramsay. His show is very popular. Viewers love to tune in and watch him heap abuse on his underlings. In fact, Chef Ramsey's disrespectful and insulting behaviour drew so many viewers that the Food Network gave him a second show, *Ramsay's Kitchen Nightmares*. In this new series, he has expanded his targets beyond kitchen staff to everyone from the restaurant owners to servers.

In *Ramsay's Kitchen Nightmares*, Chef Ramsay overhauls failing restaurants that don't know how to cook food or serve clients properly. The moment he enters the scene, everyone else is welcomed into Chef's Ramsay's nightmare challenge as he whips staff and everything else into winning shape.

The message is direct: Bullying produces results. Let's be perfectly clear. Workplace bullying is fundamentally disrespectful. Despite that, it remains prevalent due to the fundamentally flawed belief that Chef Ramsay embodies: that it makes an organization more profitable.

No one pretends Chef Ramsay is a nice guy. He insults, screams, degrades and bullies. As a result, everyone around him is stressed and fearful. In the end, however, he gets the job done. Those sous-chefs endure hell, but they learn how to turn out first-class dishes. The restaurant owners endure a nightmare, but in the end they get a profitable restaurant with patrons lining up at the door. You know the old expression: The ends justify the means.

Chef Ramsay's shows demonstrate how pervasive the legacy of command and control culture is in our workplaces. The culture exists in organizations that cannot trace a direct link to militaristic culture, as can airlines, policing and fire services.

Positional power is very hierarchical in a kitchen. The chef is the boss. He/she commands everyone in the kitchen – maybe even front-of-house staff – and if they want to stay employed, they must do as he or she says. The chef is basically commander in chief.

A number of years ago I was a member of a sexual harassment panel. Not surprisingly, most of the participants were women and the majority worked in the restaurant industry. We heard story after story about workplace abuse, much of it gender related and all of it abuse of power. These women experienced an unfortunate combination of sexual harassment and workplace bullying.

When we asked them why they did not take action, we learned that those who had tried had been effectively "blackballed" within the restaurant community. Laws or no laws, these women found themselves powerless to influence a disrespectful restaurant owner's behaviour. Their only option was to try to find other work.

The Namies' study shows that more than eighty percent of bullied individuals who file a complaint end up losing their jobs. Some are fired, and many quit to escape the abuse. Only seven percent of the bullied individuals in the study worked in companies that took action to deal with the bully. Bullying does not occur in isolation; a system supports and condones it, and that makes the system directly responsible.

Have you heard the expression "nice guys finish last?" No one goes into business to finish last. We go into business to make money. Which is why some employers reason that if they have to bully employees to do that, well, so be it. After all, if bullying was really problematic, it would be against the law, right?

Which brings me to the second reason workplace bullying remains prevalent. In most of Canada and the U.S., no law requires employers to deal with workplace-bullying complaints the way they must respond to complaints of discriminatory harassment. In Canada, we currently define unlawful disrespectful behaviour as discriminatory behaviour – involving race, gender, age or another personal characteristic protected by law.

No external body supports bullied employees. Oh sure, bullying victims can try to tell someone in the workplace about it. But as countless employees have discovered, complaining about bullying at work rarely stops it. In fact, it often makes the situation worse.

Employees who observe a co-worker being bullied are often wary they will become the next target. That, in a nutshell, is why co-workers who are asked to support a bully victim tend to back the bully boss rather than their co-worker – as research by the Namies has shown. Co-workers are even more hesitant to take that bully on when senior management seems to support the bully. While you won't find it on any mission statement, when fear dominates the workplace, it becomes a core cultural value.

We already know one reason senior management supports bullies is they value the short-term business results bullies often deliver. The lack of legal obligations should an employee complain facilitates that reality. A third reason is that bullies rarely bully "up" in the hierarchy. Senior managers rarely see the behaviour that has the bully's subordinates running for cover. So the bully's superiors generally have a more favourable perspective on the bullying manager. Their personal experience with the bully leads them to downplay or discount the complaints; they give the bully the benefit of the doubt.

In my experience, most senior managers rely on the impressions they have of the bully based on their relationship with him/her, not on observations about how that bully treats those beneath him or her. In some cases, they may have a longstanding relationship and have never seen any indication of problematic behaviour. I have no doubt that it was the relationship that senior executives had with the bully boss in that satellite office that caused them to have doubts about the complaints of the female employees.

Very few bully bosses are as overtly bullying as Chef Ramsay. Workplace bullying is typically more subtle and covert. It includes putdowns, belittling comments, name-calling, constant criticism, blame, sabotage, stealing credit, cutting the target out of the communication loop, making unreasonable job demands, criticizing the target's abilities, excluding targeted employees from meetings and relevant information, teasing, verbal abuse, blame, humiliation, monopolizing supplies, gossip, "ghost" gripes that are not true, personal and professional denigration, manipulation of job specifications, aggressive emails or notes, professional exclusion or isolation, and sabotage of career and financial status. In fact, bullies are often hard to identify because they operate "under cover." That is, on the surface they appear to be civil and cooperative, while they do everything in their power to undermine those they target for destruction.[7]

Typically, bullies are very clever and manipulative. The face they present to their own bosses is charming, solicitous and agreeable. Even when given evidence through my written reports, senior leaders often rely on their own experiences, their own relationship with the bullying manager. They believe the bullying manager, who discounts what was written in the report and discredits the employee's evidence as fabrications and lies. He or she implies that the employees are the problem.

Once I was working on a complaint where the employees had recently been assigned a new female director. The man who hired me to investigate told me she was efficient, results oriented and prepared to deal with tough issues, in contrast to the previous director. "She is also," he added, "a bit like a bull in a china shop. But overall, I have a lot of confidence in her. She's good at her job."

Now, I don't know about you, but when I think about a bull in a china shop, I imagine brute force, power, chaos and destruction. Apparently my client had a more benevolent perspective on bulls and the damage they can do when surrounded by breakable objects, like china – or a human spirit.

After interviewing some of the employees, I learned they regarded her as a bully. Most were afraid of her. They described her as outspoken, disrespectful and bossy, and they were very concerned. They were fearful to approach her about anything.

After the employee interviews, when I met with my client to debrief, I shared this information with him.

"Oh, no," he responded. "She doesn't bully the employees. She's just someone who makes sure things get done." While he conceded she might be a bit rough around the edges, he assured me she had a good heart and was promoting the best interests of the employees. I noticed he rejected any evidence I shared with him. He made excuses for each situation, or attributed the problem to the misperceptions of the employees.

As I walked back to my car, I realized that I had provided fairly pervasive evidence supporting the problematic behaviours of the director – behaviours that amounted to workplace bullying, but to no avail.

I decided that two major factors were influencing his perspective. One was his position of power. Not only was he high up in the organization, but he was a white male. He himself may never have been on the receiving end of seriously disrespectful behaviour, such as discriminatory harassment or bullying. If he had been, he might have been more understanding. The other factor influencing his response was his belief that his workplace culture was fundamentally respectful. He told me so directly and openly, and I am certain he was sincere. No doubt all his subordinates treated him respectfully, but that doesn't add up to a respectful workplace. He was top of the heap. Until I showed up, no one had told him that his experience was not everyone's experience. And of course, we already know why no one had told him about it – they were afraid. The fear that bullying creates in a workplace prevents issues and concerns from being raised.

This fellow had a personal relationship with the alleged bully. On the other hand, he had little if any relationship with her subordinates, the employees with whom I had been speaking. His impression of them was largely influenced by what his manager told him. Therefore, when presented with information that challenged his perspective, his natural tendency was to discount that information and rely on his own experience.

A comment I often hear when delivering human rights training is that "white men don't get it." People who say that mean that white male executives can interpret information only through their own experiential lens, and they are less likely to have been on the receiving end of discriminatory behaviour.

A woman who works for a large corporation recently told me over lunch about a male colleague who asked her if she thought there was anything to the notion of a "glass ceiling" (the concept that women climbing the corporate ladder are stymied by invisible barriers related to sexism). She was incredulous he would even ask such a question; we both laughed.

All this is part of the cultural disconnect between organizational and societal power, and our own personal perspective. I fully appreciate this executive's perspective but I believe in encouraging executives to question the accuracy of their points of view. I knew beyond doubt that this executive's flawed perspective could end up being very costly to his organization. I wanted to say, "Hey, wake up and smell the coffee! You have a problem in your workplace and you need to deal with it. If you don't, you may soon not have much of a workplace." The bottom line is that bullying is bad for business in the long term.

The Danger of Disrespect – The Costs of Workplace Bullying

Now that the media is placing more attention on workplace bullying, it is becoming clear that short-term gain equals long-term pain.

The website of the Canadian Centre for Occupational Health and Safety highlights the costs of workplace bullying based on information from its *Violence in the Workplace Prevention* and *Workplace Wellness* guides.

> "Workplace bullies create a tremendous liability for the employer by causing stress-related health and safety problems, and driving good employees out of the organization.
>
> Bullied employees waste between ten and fifty-two percent of their time at work…defending themselves and networking for support, thinking about the situation [and] being demotivated and stressed, not to mention taking sick leave due to stress-related illnesses.
>
> Bullies poison their working environment with low morale, fear, anger and depression. The employer pays for this in lost efficiency, absenteeism, high staff turnover, severance packages and lawsuits. In extreme cases, a violent incident may be the tragic outcome.
>
> The target's family and friends also suffer the results of daily stress and eventual breakdown. Marriages suffer or are destroyed under the pressure of the target's anxiety and anger. Friendships cool because the bullied employee becomes obsessive about the situation.
>
> Moreover, our health care system ends up repairing the damage: visits to the doctor for symptoms of stress, prescriptions for antidepressants, and long-term counselling or psychiatric care. In this sense, we all pay."

While the Canadian Centre for Occupational Health and Safety has not put an actual cost on the amount we all pay, we know it is a lot. Australian researcher Paul McCarthy estimates that overall, workplace bullying costs Canadian companies close to $20,000 per employee per year.[8]

We hear a lot these days about employee engagement. Rightly so. Engaged employees produce better business results. Ask yourself how engaged employees can be if they spend ten to fifty-two percent of their work time dealing with the effects of being bullied. How engaged can they be if they are fearful, angry or depressed because of a toxic work atmosphere poisoned by bullying? We don't even need to ask how engaged employees can be when the bullying behaviour culminates in a medical leave. Such employees certainly are "engaged" – just not in a way that promotes business success and profitability. They are focused instead on coping with the disrespectful behaviour.

Not convinced yet? Here's what the U.S.-based Bullying.com has to say about the cost of workplace bullying:

"Long-term costs to the organization include health care costs, legal costs, time lost in preparing or attending court cases, a reduction in productivity and the expense associated with replacing staff. The less visible yet still significant costs associated with workplace bullying include the time and expense of internal employee complaints, mediation, adverse publicity, the loss of talent, lower morale among employees, absenteeism, reduction of efficiency, productivity and profitability, loss of collective wisdom and experience, and a damaged public image that may make it more difficult to attract key talent in the future."[9]

So, while fear may be an effective motivator and may accelerate job performance in the short term, the inverse is true over the longer term. A host of negative organizational consequences exists when employees work in a fear-based culture.

Let's spend a moment talking about the ability to attract key talent. I've mentioned before that in a tight labour market – where there are more jobs than job seekers – employees gain some power.

When the opposite is true – there are more job seekers than jobs – employers may be "lucky"; they may be like that bully-employer in the small town whose female employees felt trapped and wouldn't quit regardless of how he treated them.

But if long-term thinking takes into account a tight labour market – and we all know that as Baby Boomers retire, demographics have pushed us in that direction – such behaviour is sure to produce a negative outcome.

Remember the talented summer student we met in Chapter Two? After several months in the disrespectful workplace culture of her summer job, she decided she would never return. That's the more common scenario. Given a choice, valuable employees choose to work where they feel safe, comfortable, respected and valued. This is not open for debate – it is fact.

Due to the pace of change in our techno-based world, employers needn't wait long to find themselves facing this situation. The power shift brought on by the ever-shrinking labour pool has combined with a growing awareness of workplace bullying. More and more bullied victims – from the Namies to Helen Green – are coming out of the shadows, getting vocal, trying to force their employers to make changes. Put "workplace bullying" into your search engine and you'll see how available information on the topic has become. As awareness grows, more and more employees recognize and confront it. Knowledge yields personal power. Bullied employees are increasingly likely to leave an organization that condones bullying.

One of the better websites on the topic is called *No Bully For Me* (www.nobullyforme.org). It supports victims of workplace bullying. "Greetings," the home page begins. "This site is created and run by Stephen and Karen, two former targets of workplace bullying; we do know what it's like. In these pages you will find help, advice and information to protect yourself, inform yourself and take steps to heal your situation."

No Bully For Me, like Ruth and Gary Namie's efforts in the U.S., and the late Tim Fields' in Britain, is founded by individuals who have personally experienced workplace bullying. Its goal is to educate, support and assist other workplace victims.

No Bully For Me operates as a support group where targets can share their experiences with other victims of workplace bullying. *No Bully For Me* has established support groups in locations throughout British Columbia. A participant in one of my bullying workshops recently told me that being able to attend one of these meetings was a cathartic experience. She realized it wasn't just she who suffered! When she heard participants' stories and learned about practical strategies that had worked for others, it completely changed her perspective. She walked in feeling defeated, but left feeling empowered.

I started this chapter with a quote from Louis Maltby of National Workrights Institute, who in 2001 compared the issue of workplace bullying with that of sexual harassment twenty years earlier. One similarity is the gender factor: research shows that, as with sexual harassment, women are targeted in the majority of workplace bullying complaints.

While sexual harassment is now against the law just about everywhere in the industrial world, this was not always the case. Gender discrimination is as old as Adam and Eve. When I became pregnant while working at the airline, I asked my human resources advisor to set up maternity benefits for me. At some point during what I considered a routine administrative process, she looked up and said, "You don't know how lucky you are. When I had my kids, I lost my job. All three times."

My first thought was that she didn't seem that old. In fact, she had entered the workplace in the late 1960s or early 1970s, along with many other women. Few women then had probably heard the term "sexual harassment," yet by the mid-1970s, the rising number of court cases involving discrimination against women spawned the term's definition – and the first laws prohibiting that behaviour. Sexual harassment became a legal issue for employers in Canada in 1977 when Parliament adopted the Canadian Human Rights Act, which prohibited sexual discrimination in employment.

So, while workplace bullying is currently not a legal issue in most of Canada or the U.S., that will likely change in the very near future. Quebec started the ball rolling in 1994 when it coined the term "psychological harassment" and created a statutory obligation for employers to deal with that behaviour under its labour standards legislation. (Statutory obligation is the legal obligation for employers to deal with complaints of discrimination in Canadian workplaces.) Quebec employers have that same legal obligation with respect to complaints of workplace bullying.

As of June 2008, so do employers that are federally regulated. Federal Labour Minister Jean-Pierre Blackburn announced new regulations which will require companies in the federal jurisdiction to develop policies to prevent "workplace violence, including bullying, teasing or abusive behaviour."[10] As well, federally regulated employers will have to provide staff training and monitor the effectiveness of their anti-bullying policies.

While Quebec has retained that harassment label, psychological harassment is defined as "any vexatious behaviour in the form of repeated and hostile or unwanted conduct, verbal comments, actions or gestures, that affects an employee's dignity or psychological or physical integrity and that results in a harmful work environment for the employee."

If we compare that to definitions of workplace bullying, clearly psychological harassment is synonymous with workplace bullying. The language in the Quebec legislation refers to intentional, ongoing behaviour that results in harm to the employee. It may be called psychological harassment, but this was in fact the first Canadian anti-bullying legislation, and is recognized as such both in Canada and internationally. In 2007, Saskatchewan introduced Bill 66, an amendment to the Occupational Health and Safety Act. Bill 66 also refers to harassment, which is broadly defined to encompass workplace bullying as behaviour that constitutes a threat to the health and safety of a worker.

Saskatchewan's Bill 66 is in keeping with legislative trends in the European Union, Australia and New Zealand, where workplace bulling is increasingly recognized as a health and safety issue. It is the element of harm that influences this legislative direction.

This changing legal landscape will continue to affect that

employer/employee power shift to which I referred earlier. However, in the interim, many targeted employees will not wait until their legislators require employers to deal with workplace bullying. Armed with knowledge about the issue, they are already demanding changes in their workplaces. When they raise their complaints with employers and those employers fail to take appropriate action, they start to explore legal options under Canadian law. As Helen Green's employer learned when her case ended in a $1.7 million settlement, the options available can be very costly.

Bullied employees can file civil suits against their employers. They can claim constructive dismissal or wrongful dismissal, and ask for damages. In a constructive dismissal claim, employees argue that they were forced to quit their job by their employer's actions, or in the case of workplace bullying, lack of action. These claims arise because any employee can argue there has been a breach of the common law employment contract that exists between employee and employer. The common law employment contract applies to all working relationships in every workplace. Since 2000, part of it obliges an employer to treat an employee with civility, dignity and respect. In 2000, the Ontario Court of Appeal released a decision that equated bullying-type mistreatment with repudiation of the entire employment contract.[11] This set a precedent for individuals claiming they are forced to quit by the bullying behaviour they experience at work.

This means an employee who can prove he/she was forced to quit his/her job because of workplace bullying, and can prove that the employer did nothing to deal with it, can file a constructive dismissal suit. If that employee is fired from his/her job due to workplace bullying, he/she can file a wrongful dismissal suit.

Canadian employees can also file tort suits against their employer – claims concerned with the intentional or negligent infliction of harm. Because ongoing bullying at work causes harm, employers should not underestimate an employee's ability to go down that path.

An important distinction between discriminatory harassment

and workplace bullying is that the former is heard in an administrative tribunal system, while the latter is heard in civil courts. Traditionally, damage awards for the human rights cases are low. Tribunals use an unofficial $20,000 cap as a guide when awarding damages. But more recent decisions indicate that the cap is moving up; we are starting to see damage awards in the $24,000 range on a routine basis.

These pale in comparison to the awards for complaints that go through the civil courts. In recent years, two cases of disrespectful behaviour have caused the business community to sit up and take notice – the Keays decision and the Sulz decision.

In the 2005 Keays decision, the Ontario Supreme Court awarded Kevin Keays monetary compensation equivalent to twenty-four months' notice as well as $500,000 in punitive damages. Keays, a fourteen-year employee, had filed a wrongful dismissal suit against his former employer, Honda. Keays developed post traumatic stress disorder and quit his job after experiencing what the court termed "callous and insensitive treatment" at the hands of his employer.[12] In 2006, the court also granted Keays a whopping $610,000 in legal costs. On appeal, Honda managed to reduce the damage award to $100,000. Still, Honda probably had to apply the money it got back toward its very costly legal bill.

In 2006, the BC Supreme Court followed the example of the Keays decision and awarded Nancy Sulz, a former RCMP officer, $950,000 in damages due to the psychological damage she suffered at the hands of her commanding officer. His bullying was so severe it caused medical experts to conclude that Sulz would never be able to work full time again. This time, the appeals court upheld the original damages amount.[13]

Speaking at a meeting of the Canadian Association for the Prevention of Discrimination and Harassment in Higher Education, Madam Justice Freda Steel of the Manitoba Court of Appeal stated, "Now more and more the law is looking not only to prevent discrimination based on affiliation with a particular group, but is also looking to control inappropriate behaviour on a personal level.

I see more situations where the law is saying, 'No, you can't treat people that way; you can't talk to people that way.'"[14]

It is only a matter of time before we are at the same legal point with workplace bullying as we were thirty years ago with sexual harassment. Other governments in Canada will be following the lead of Quebec, Saskatchewan and the federal jurisdiction and will pass legislation to make workplace bullying a legal issue for all employers in Canada.

That gives employers a choice: to wait until the law forces them to deal with workplace bullying, or to take heed of the data that proves it has severe and long-lasting negative effects on an organization's bottom line. Employers who worship at the shrine of Chef Ramsay believe the end justifies the means, that ignoring (i.e. supporting) bullying inevitably leads to organizational success and profitability. How many more studies like those I've listed need to come out before employers realize this is a dangerous myth?

In business, the ultimate goal is success, defined as profitability. If there is no profit, there is no business. I am fully behind businesses making a profit; I just don't believe that bullying people equates with profitability. Adopting respect as a core value leads to profits. When companies live by that value, they don't condone or tolerate bullying behaviour.

I asked successful Employers of Choice two questions: Do you have human rights, harassment or bullying policies? And do you keep data and/or statistics on the numbers of complaints you process?

"What people are accountable for," replied Val Duffey, HR director at KPMG, "is the respectful, tolerant, diverse behaviour, and we measure that in the environment. We (at our level in HR) have not had to really swoop in. There are always some individual employee relationship situations. We have seen bullying the odd time. But the situations are so few and far between. They don't happen because they are at odds with the culture. It just wouldn't be tolerated."

As I tell my clients, a respectful workplace is one where, by definition, issues of discrimination, harassment and bullying occur with far less frequency because they are at odds with the established organizational culture and values. In a respectful workplace culture, when complaints do arise, they are dealt with quickly and locally, minimizing organization disruption and associated costs.

Employers of Choice all have policies for harassment and bullying, even though they don't have cause to use them often. All actively solicit feedback on an ongoing basis. As a result, they generally know about situations before those concerns develop into problems.

Interestingly, too, while Employers of Choice have hierarchical power positions, bullying behaviours are conspicuously absent from the leadership lexicon. That's because leaders are expected to direct employees in a respectful manner, and are held accountable for doing so. Just as managerial bullying results in a fear-based culture, a respectful workplace stems from a respectful managerial approach.

Employers of Choice are after the same result – business success – as companies that subscribe to the Chef Ramsay approach. They're simply more likely to achieve it in the long term. Respectful collaborative leadership results in successful businesses. The proof is in the profits.

7

Respectful Leadership

All decisions are made with the interests of the employees doing the work in mind, and in an effort to make people feel respected, confident and free to do whatever it takes to make guests happy.

—ELLEN DU BELLAY, vice president of learning and development, Four Seasons Hotels

M Y BOSS AT the airline managed us in a respectful manner. At the time, however, I never thought about it. I just knew I really liked working for her.

She never made me feel I was her subordinate. Although she was at least two levels above me, I always felt we were colleagues. She consulted with me about work-related issues relevant to my job. She took time to discuss matters with me and was never too busy when I needed to talk to her, despite the fact that she worked long days with neither lunches nor breaks.

She also made sure that I didn't feel guilty leaving before her at the end of the work day. Prior to my job with her I had been a professional dancer. I was used to physical activity and felt challenged by this new situation that involved sitting for long stretches of time. By about three o'clock every afternoon, I was itching to get up and move around. I always attended a late afternoon fitness class after work.

My boss was clear about her expectation that the work get done – and done well. However, she trusted us to accomplish that in whatever manner suited each of us. For me, that meant coming in early so I could leave in time for my fitness class.

I never recall being afraid to speak to her, despite being awed at times by her cleverness and capability. During my first year's steep learning curve, I was constantly in her office, asking advice or accessing her wealth of knowledge.

She regularly told me that she wanted me to succeed, and provided ongoing feedback on my job performance.

She was like this even though the airline's culture did not require management to lead respectfully. Some managers promoted respect and empowerment; others did not. When my reporting relationship changed, so did my entire experience of my work environment.

Such variations in managerial style do not exist when an organization makes a conscious decision to adopt respect as a core organizational value. A respectful workplace culture boasts consistency in leadership style. Everyone leads in a respectful manner. They have no choice.

One reason for the consistency is that employees are encouraged to raise work-related issues, including problematic behaviours on the part of managers. In such a culture, employees are not afraid to express themselves.

"Bullying behaviour might happen, but I think people would call their manager on it," says Carolynne Warner, manager of human resources at SaskTel. "Some might say it directly, some might go to the union, but it would not be put up with. There is not a high tolerance level for inappropriate communications."

Another reason for the consistency: in a respectful workplace culture, individuals in positions of power understand they are expected to act in a certain way, and will be monitored and evaluated on whether they do.

"It is really about treating others the way we want to be treated, and there is a very high level of intolerance for the opposite," says Four Season's vice president of learning and development, Ellen du Bellay. "We don't fire people for technical skills. We fire them if they are not respectful. We do an employee survey every other year and a management opinion survey every year. [Our decision makers include] line staff, management staff and executive staff. We ask our employees about the executive team each year. The executive team is under a lot of scrutiny. We have terminated people for consistent disrespect of people."

Employers of Choice design managerial training to ensure a consistency of respectful leadership. Managers are taught to create an open-door environment.

Besides giving managers ongoing and appropriate training in leading respectfully, Employers of Choice ensure that all employees, including managers, are treated respectfully when they have work-related challenges.

As Jane Sillberg, director of human resources at Intuit Canada says, "Let us say we have a new manager who is having a difficult issue. The HR business partner will support them ... being there at the meeting or coaching beforehand. This is on all levels. I coach the executive levels so they get the skills, and we help them to direct the conversation. And once you have coached them, it becomes the way they behave."

When respect permeates a workplace culture, there's an absence of fear among employees; they are not afraid to speak out, because they are actively encouraged to do so. And when they do speak out, they are treated with respect. They are not ignored, ridiculed or intimidated. They can see that their feedback is valued and considered. They are included in the communication loop.

Likewise, managers are not afraid to admit when they are having difficulties. They are taught to get the help they need when they need it, that doing so is essential to the success of the business. Asking for help is not seen as a sign of weakness or incompetence. Managers are trained, supported and empowered to lead through collaboration and respect. Respectful relationships are encouraged and trust is developed throughout the organization, regardless of where an employee works or how much power they hold. The result is win/win for employees, managers and the bottom line.

"People deserve to be treated respectfully," says Sillberg. "Your practices must demonstrate that you support them and trust them. If you run your company from a non-trusting point of view, how do you show respect? I have worked in organizations with really nice people who treat their staff badly," Sillberg continued. "I have found throughout my career that you can work with people who are great people, but they don't behave toward people properly because that is the culture. When I came to Intuit, I was surprised to see how respectful everyone was. You still have the conversation, but it is a different conversation. It is a different tone, with different body language."

When all the leaders in an organization truly embrace respect, employees feel safe, empowered and respected. Rather than being motivated by fear, employees are motivated by a sense of pride and commitment to their work, team and organization. Respectful leadership spawns a workforce that is truly engaged and focused on promoting the success of the business.

Respectful Complaint Handling –
Accessibility, Availability and Accountability

I have been writing Respectful Workplace policies for employers for more than a decade. When I started my practice, I naïvely assumed that if I wrote a good policy, employees would use it when they had a complaint. I met with clients to design effective complaint resolution processes. It took me years to realize that it was workplace culture, not the quality of my policies, that determined whether employees bothered to read and use them.

When employees are bullied or harassed, they tend to do one of three things. They a) do nothing – just put up with it, or b) take a leave of absence (sometimes medical) or c) quit. Very few look at their company's policy to see what form their complaint should take.

I had been at my airline job for three months when I arrived at work one day to find an ad ripped out of a magazine on my desk. It was for a *Buns of Steel* video and it featured a woman's buttocks prominently displayed in a thong leotard. I'd only just spotted it when I realized that two of my male colleagues were standing at my door, observing me with smiles. I looked over and asked, "Hey, what is this, guys?"

One of them, a manager in the labour department in charge of training me in my new position, told me that he and a union VP had been on a plane together the day before, when they had seen the ad in a magazine and thought of me.

I was in a new job, still on probation and working on a union portfolio amongst mostly males. Whether their message was that my behind was flabby and needed the *Buns of Steel* video, or whether they thought I had a Buns of Steel backside, I instantly viewed this incident as problematic.

I knew I should say something to them that very moment, something that would prevent future "tests" of this kind. Or I should have said something a little later to each of them in the privacy of their offices. I should have asked them their intentions or told them how their "joke" made me feel. However, that is not the choice I made. I smiled back at them, made some joking comment, put the ad in my desk drawer and never told anyone about the incident.

Why? I didn't want to risk the fallout. I was already different from my colleagues, who were overwhelmingly male and lifetime airline employees. Like most people, I desperately wanted to fit in and be part of the group. In male-dominated environments, acceptance often involves ribbing and joking. They frame the joking as harmless and all in good fun even when it is disparaging and related to personal characteristics like sex, nationality and sexual orientation – all three of which are protected grounds in human rights law.

Such jokes were typical of the airline's culture, "the way it is around here." I didn't want to be labelled a prude or someone who couldn't take a joke. So even if didn't like it, I'd already figured out it was best to "put up and shut up," a phrase I have heard numerous times from employees on the receiving end of disrespectful behaviour. I figured this was something I'd have to learn to deal with if I was going to continue to work there.

I have seen countless variations of that experience in my consulting practice. Employees don't speak up because the message they have gotten, either overtly or covertly, is that it's better not to. They are scared of what will happen if they raise an issue. They are worried they will be excluded. They suspect they will be labelled a troublemaker or whiner. They believe others will use their complaint as fodder for more joking. Basically, they are fearful that saying something will encourage more individuals to target them.

Even those who speak to a manager, commonly identified as the "go to" person in organizational policies, often find things get worse instead of better. And if an employee's manager is the problem (or part of it), what then? It was a manager who put that ad on my desk. Like many people in this position, I found the power issue a deterrent against acting. In such instances, the only real option is to go over the manager's head, to his or her boss or to human resources. However, employees often sense that going over their manager's head is frowned upon, which makes them fearful to act. Those that do find that the process inevitably involves the same manager they are complaining about, leading to an even worse situation at work. Regardless of organizational policy, employees often get the message that complaints will be handled in a way that either produces no resolution, or will make things worse.

Happily, this is not the case at Employers of Choice workplaces, as confirmed by Robert Watson, president and CEO of SaskTel. I initially wrote Watson to request an interview for this book so that I could divulge SaskTel's policies. Unlike with other interview requests (where it took a series of phone calls to be referred to the appropriate representative), I got a phone call from Watson himself shortly after speaking with an administrative assistant.

He promptly started answering my questions about how SaskTel promotes respect as a core cultural value. I also spoke with Caro-lynne Warner, manager of human resources at SaskTel.

"We have an open door policy that truly comes from the executive down," Warner said. "Anyone has an opportunity to send anything they want to ask directly to Robert, or they can talk to their man-ager or their vp. Employees have the opportunity to express their concerns." She added that when employees contact Watson, they always receive a personal response from him, just as I did.

Watson doesn't always wait for employees to come to him. He creates opportunities for employees to meet and talk with him. Watson tours the province regularly, giving employees updates on what is going on in the organization during informal meetings with open sessions at which participants are encouraged to ask whatever they want. Employees are not required to attend. These sessions are considered "part of the business process" at SaskTel, one of many vehicles for collecting feedback.

Think about the message employees get when told the CEO is coming to visit with a state-of-the-company update including a question-and-answer session. Although Watson is in SaskTel's ultimate power position, the firm offers no evidence of a command and control leadership style. Like the other CEOs at Employers of Choice workplaces, Watson models respectful leadership, actively encouraging two-way communication with his entire firm, and empowering employees to discuss issues with him directly.

Now, I bet you're wondering how Watson gets any work done. You're thinking he must be swamped and overwhelmed dealing with employee issues. You're wondering why he even has an HR depart-ment. In reality, however, employees don't usually go straight to the top with issues or concerns. Employees are more likely to use these opportunities to "express an interest in an opportunity, or a concern about a direction that they see, or a business issue," says Warner.

From the moment they start their career at SaskTel, employees get a very clear message. They are part of an organization that wants them to be involved and to express themselves. It stems from SaskTel's core value of respect. "When employees feel like they are being treated with respect, it develops a healthy environment which results in them being engaged," says Warner. "In the early 1990s we didn't talk about being engaged. Being respectful was part of developing a healthy workplace. It was about treating people with respect and with integrity and providing them with honest information – the whole notion of each member of the team being encouraged and allowed to participate to the level of their abilities. It is about employees having a say, and ensuring that ideas from employees are being sought out."

The opportunity for a SaskTel employee to meet with the president is just one of a myriad of options available when he or she has questions, concerns or feedback about the workplace. "Different departments have different mechanisms," says Warner. "In some departments, the VP comes to a meeting so that employees can ask questions. It is all about creating that feedback loop. The executives do make a point to be available to their whole area and to be seen on a regular basis so that there is the ability to have a conversation."

What a contrast to my experience back at the airline. There, the CEO would tour the operations centre once a year, right before Christmas. We would all wait quietly in our offices. He would come around, led by our departmental VP, say Merry Christmas or Happy Holidays, and go off to the next office. That was the only time I ever saw him. Other than that, he confined himself to the executive wing. While there were initiatives encouraging employees to submit ideas, these were formal, written processes with rules and forms. The notion of being able to go directly to the CEO and have a chat was unheard of in that culture.

Watson's leadership style at SaskTel encourages neither a fear-based culture nor disrespectful behaviours. His leadership style encourages a participative and expressive culture where employees are empowered to raise and resolve issues.

Employees hear about SaskTel's respectful practices in their first recruitment interview. And once employees start working in a team, they experience the corporate values in action. Regardless of where an employee works, the manager is in close communication with each employee, providing feedback and getting feedback. It is set up so that employees can express themselves.

At SaskTel, Watson's leadership style permeates all levels of management. Managers are trained to create collaborative teams, and are held accountable for doing so. Like at KPMG, SaskTel uses its employee survey to gather feedback about both managerial and executive performance. "On our employee survey, we ask about the employee's immediate manager," says Warner. "Each department gets the results from their own employees. It lets each department see what their employees are saying about leadership and fair treatment. When we get the employee survey results back, each department looks at their results and puts a concrete action plan in place to improve any areas that need improvement. Often all of the employees are included in the development of those actions. Every department is required to do this."

Developing an action plan based on employee feedback is considered essential at SaskTel. It is a business requirement.

Just as leaders are held accountable for their behaviour, so is each and every employee. Employees are actively involved in translating the corporate values into behaviour. Teams of employees are assigned to examine the values and decide what behaviours do or don't demonstrate these values. Leaders do this with teams. "So if I see a team member who does not demonstrate the corporate values, I need to ask myself, what is my response?" says Warner. "A response can be individualized, because each team's culture is slightly different... This process gives people the tools and the permission to hold each other accountable."

The bottom line is that accountability is woven into the fabric of the workplace culture at SaskTel. Employees are provided with communication and conflict resolution tools so they can deal with issues as they arise. While the culture encourages open communication, it doesn't mean employees can voice anything on their minds. What they express must be honest and respectful.

Employees in such environments are required to make a choice different than I made that day I saw the *Buns of Steel* advertisement on my desk. SaskTel demands that employees take action when they have an issue, concern or conflict. That's simply "the way it is."

Says Warner, "We expect that there will be conflict, but we also expect that it will be dealt with. If I see you demonstrating a lack of respect, as your team member I am responsible to bring it to your attention."

If that doesn't work, employees talk to their manager or follow a variety of other avenues available, including going over heads to approach an executive.

When I asked Warner of SaskTel about complaint statistics, she echoed what I'd heard from the other Employers of Choice. The more her firm offers conflict resolution training and encouragement to bring forward concerns, the fewer complaints, or even concerns, it sees. "Conflicts are being addressed earlier than they may have been in the past."

Given the similarities in leadership practices at Employers of Choice, there is clearly a wealth of information available for firms just embarking on the Road to Respectful Leadership. The key is to become familiar with best practices and assess which would best suit your particular situation, then adapt and apply those in a manner likely to work. As SaskTel's experience indicates, it's crucial that they filter down to the micro level, shaped along the way to reflect the culture of each team.

One consistent feature is the accessibility and availability of the people in positions of power, which better enables them to build relationships with their teams. That, in turn, establishes the trust necessary for creating an environment in which employees feel safe to talk about their issues. According to Cliff Yeo, human resources advisor for the BC region at Canada Safeway, "If you have a concern, you can go to a mentor, the department manger, store manager, HR advisor, union business agent or to EAP. And it is encouraged… Managers do whatever they can to foster that environment where employees want to come to them."

On their first day at Safeway, new employees receive a welcome card from the store manager. On the front cover it says, "Welcome to Safeway." The inside reads, "At Safeway, we pride ourselves in providing world class service to those who walk through our doors every day. We also strive to provide the best working environment for our employees. I would like to formally welcome you to our team. Feedback regarding any of your training and/or orientation into the workplace is appreciated. Should you have any questions, comments or concerns, please don't hesitate to speak with me at any time or, as an added resource, your human resources advisor (phone number provided).

Signed by the employee's store manager, the card is followed up by a personal meeting with that manager. The meeting aims to build a relationship and reinforce the message that at Safeway, the culture encourages employees to raise issues and give leaders feedback.

The store manager then actively works to develop that relationship. Each store manager has an open-door policy. Most managers will do a tour of the store on a regular basis, to say hello to all the staff. Most try to go for coffee with different people. They have team huddles, as well as one-on-one meetings with employees.

Scott Gibney, public affairs manager for Canada Safeway, told me, "In all of the jobs I have had, I have never seen the inclusiveness I have seen at Safeway. Our CEO in Canada started as a baggage boy. Most of our executive team also started that way. I knew my VP as Mike before I knew him as the VP. It is a family, very tight-knit, relationship-based. We play baseball, golf, have parties. We have a program around charitable giving called Safeway We Care. Each store chooses its own initiative. We hold an appreciation gala in each store. All the executive team attends and they personally go and thank everyone."

Respectful behaviour is encouraged through fostering relationships across hierarchical power levels. Employees and managers both have relationships with executives; it creates a completely different organizational dynamic than in traditional cultures. Transparency, accountability and cohesion are encouraged; disrespectful behaviour and abuse of power – so characteristic of command and control cultures – is discouraged.

Like at SaskTel and Safeway, Four Seasons promotes respect through relationship-building. By the time an employee begins work at a Four Seasons hotel, they have already met their department manager, hotel manager and the general manager. The day they start work, they meet an HR representative. "We have this unwritten rule about management-by-walking-around," says Ellen du Bellay. "A lot of our HR team spend most of their time walking around. Relationships build over time. HR is very much involved with the life of the employee at the hotel. We think about the HR team as the conscience of the hotel. Each member of the HR team gets to know the employees in the hotel. They know each employee's name, and often their families."

From the outset, employees receive a myriad of messages confirming they are part of a team. Leaders are involved and visible. Their behaviour demonstrates the core value of respect, the cornerstone of the Four Seasons Golden Rule culture. Says du Bellay, "We make a big deal of using our guests' names, so we also make a big deal about management knowing and using employees' names. The executives come in at night so that they can interact with the overnight crew. When there is a crunch, a call goes out for anyone to help. Managers will come in and bus tables, and then there will be celebrations at the end."

Celebrating success and encouraging social interaction are very effective ways to build relationships and promote teamwork in a workplace. Frequent interactions ensure that HR staff get to know the hotel employees.

"HR is the social centre of the hotel," observes du Bellay. "It is always located near the employee entrance. Each hotel has a fairly healthy budget for employee relations events. We have employee picnics and holiday parties, which include families and kids. We hold an employee appreciation day where the executives serve everyone lunch." In addition to these events, each hotel has an employee-of-the-month event. When employees receive service awards, everyone is included and attends the event.

Interestingly, while all Four Seasons employees are on a first name basis with each other, du Bellay advised me that they generally refer to the general manager as Mr. or Ms. – not because the company requires it, but voluntarily because it demonstrates respect.

Relationship building across hierarchical lines ensures that employees have many people they can approach with issues or concerns. "If you are a housekeeper and want to see the general manager, you have the right to do that," du Bellay says. "We do reassure people that they have the right to do it... We also have something called Direct Line, where line staff meet with the general manager [for] a candid conversation. Usually that is a quarterly meeting; some hotels do it monthly... We don't seem to have trouble getting feedback."

If Four Seasons employees have no fear about expressing their concerns, it's directly related to the fact they don't feel fear. And that, in turn, is due to the availability and accessibility of leaders, and purposeful relationship building. Employees who don't feel comfortable with direct communication can provide feedback (including about their manager's behaviour) through the firm's organizational opinion survey. Of course, Four Seasons survey results rarely reveal a problem of which HR is not already aware. "It is shocking for us to get feedback about a manager who is not treating people right," says du Bellay. "Our culture is such that we are very protective of the employee."

At Four Seasons hotels, leaders are expected to demonstrate respectful leadership. "There is a lot of accountability there, so the manager wouldn't think of not being respectful. Role modelling and mentoring are very important to us. We have mentoring programs for every manager and that is really important."

At Intuit, there are quarterly opportunities for employees to meet with CEO Yves Millette. They're called All Hands meetings. Like other Employers of Choice, Intuit understands the importance of building relationships across hierarchical lines to empower and engage employees. Intuit Canada employees also have the opportunity to interact with the U.S. CEO at least once a year, again at All Hands meetings. All Hands meetings aim to keep employees up to date on what is happening in the company.

"It is not about boring our employees," says Jane Sillberg. "It is about engaging them. They learn about how the company is doing and then we do fun stuff to help them learn. At the last one, we had a group called Boom Makers for a team building exercise. We made music with noisemakers. The message was we are all in it together. Everyone got T-shirts. We played Beatles music, particularly the song 'Come Together.' These events remind us that we are one."

Intuit engages in a host of activities to create an inclusive, team-based culture. While the titles and executive positions are the same as those in fear-based command and control cultures, Intuit leaders demonstrate behaviour that indicates they're just part of the group, co-workers.

Says Sillberg, "Every second Thursday we have a social from three to six. Everyone is invited. It is a time when employees from different departments come together and chat. We have karaoke and everybody, even the CEO and executive group, attends."

Part of living the core value of respect includes demonstrating respect for the larger community. Employers of Choice each have their own version of the Safeway We Care program. Intuit is involved in Habitat for Humanity. "Eighty-eight percent of employees participate," says Sillberg. "We give them four paid days off. I was involved in building the House that Intuit Built. When we were involved in that project, I was just Jane, not the vice president of human resources. Getting involved in an activity like that creates a different kind of bond than we would have if we stayed in our office. So now I am just a person that they can come and talk to. This kind of activity eliminates those hierarchical perspectives that are commonly found in organizations. We really reinforce that we are all people and that we all want to help our community and give back to it. We have different jobs, but that doesn't make us better than anyone else. It feels good to see that we have made a difference in a person's life. Other organizations see it as 'how can you afford to do that?' For us it helps to bring to life the fact that we are a values-driven organization."

Intuit builds on the bonds its philanthropic activities create with a host of initiatives. Leaders being accessible, available and accountable is just "the way it is" at Intuit. "It is not about events. It is about the way you run your business," says Sillberg. "It is about mindset. It is in everything that you do. We are constantly looking for other opportunities, ways for employees to connect with us. It is not the kind of thing where we sit down and say 'what can we do?' It just comes up in conversation."

Not surprisingly, employees at Intuit have the same flexibility as those who work at other Employers of Choice when it comes to who they can approach about a work-related issue. "If an employee is having a problem with their manager, they can go to the HR person in their business unit, to their manager, to their manager's boss or to the CEO. Anyone can go to the CEO at any time. We have a thing called 'Ask Yves.' It is anonymous and employees can ask anything. The whole senior team, all sixteen of us, have regular office hours. The whole schedule is published on the internet. Everyone has different times. The times are also posted on our doors, and anyone can come and talk to us during those office hours. Our rationale is that when you are in a senior position, the reality is that you are always in meetings. It is not fair for an employee to wait when they have an issue. This forces us to be available to them."

When a senior executive says "it is not fair" for an employee to wait when they have an issue, he/she is sending a clear message. It is fundamentally respectful that the executive team makes itself available on a regular basis to any employee who wants to meet with them. It says to an employee, "You count, you matter, you are important and your concerns deserve to be addressed." Respectful leadership means leaders are accountable not only to those higher up, but to everyone in the organization.

"Senior leader chats" are another respectful leadership practice at Inuit. The idea developed from "CEO chats," which were designed to let employees talk directly to the CEO Yves Millette. Sillberg says, "As an executive team, we don't know what is going on; we are too far removed. The employees have things that they want to tell us, and because we are senior, we have the ability to make the changes. We are not arrogant enough to say, 'You are there, just keep reworking your process to make improvement.'" In this way, Inuit recognizes employees as a vital part of the success of the business.

Intuit has a traditional hierarchical power structure, as does SaskTel and other Employers of Choice. What is not traditional, however, is the way that positional power manifests within the organization. Says Sillberg, "Although we have a hierarchy, it is not viewed that way. It is a community. We also have skip-level conversations. My boss goes to my employees and asks how I am doing, and then she provides me feedback."

Jane Sillberg of Intuit advised me that she seldom hears anything from her boss that her employees have not already told her directly. "I have not yet had a surprise. I have generally already heard it from them. I am quite driven at work and my employees worry about me. They say, Jane it is time to go home."

At Intuit, employees are not afraid to express themselves. They do not get a message that they "can't go over their bosses' heads" as is true in so many command and control organizations. Leaders demonstrate that they consider themselves part of the team. Says Sillberg, "We don't just communicate through email. We have the skip level, the senior leader chats, one-on-one meetings, team meetings. We talk about what kind of communication we need, and I let my employees tell me what they need. When I first started, I needed to meet with them once a week, and then it was 'What do you need?' And then we have weekly staff meetings. We also have stand-up meetings. They are fifteen-minute meetings that can happen every day to once a week. The relevant team comes together and you talk about what is happening at the immediate time. The purpose is to remove obstacles and provide help. In season, we do them every day so people have access immediately. People literally stand up. It is to solve problems. If they have an issue they need dealt with, we want them to be able to solve that issue immediately."

Another characteristic of respectful leadership is responsiveness and flexibility. Leaders are empowered to make decisions and act quickly when necessary. This is a critically important component of ongoing organizational profitability and success, particularly in the current global business context. In the most comprehensive study of the relationship between organizational culture and profitability to date, Harvard business school professors James Heskett and John Kotter concluded that regardless of a company's short-term success, only those with adaptive cultures remain profitable over time.[1]

Respectful leadership allows an organization to react and adapt when necessary, and shows an interest in promoting business success over satisfying hierarchical procedures and bureaucratic red tape. "We are flexible in what we do," says Intuit's Sillberg. "We look at our business and we look at what is needed and we do what is appropriate. That takes time. Somebody has to make those decisions. You have to have somebody with their head above the weeds. It is a responsibility that we are all aware of."

One aspect I cherish about working for myself is not having to spend time in meetings. While I appreciate that meetings are necessary in any organization, I often find them frustrating and boring. I know I am not the only one who feels this way. At one point when I was working at the airline, we all took a course on how to structure meetings so that they would be more productive. People were given different functions in an effort to keep the meetings on track. While these ideas seemed good in theory, I found that they never worked in practice. There was no consistency in application. There was no accountability to ensure these effective meeting practices were really integrated into the organizational culture.

At one point, the labour department started to have Monday morning departmental meetings that included our VP. These meetings took hours and I was always itching to get out of them. While I appreciated the opportunity to interact with my colleagues, we would go around the table and everyone would say what they were doing and what was going on in their portfolio. While it was never overtly expressed, we all felt we had to talk about something – as if to justify that we were in fact working. Because our portfolios were distinct, I often listened to irrelevant information, but there was no opportunity to provide input on the structure of the meetings, to say whether we thought they were useful. Our VP called them and we attended. When he was out of town, the whole idea often fizzled out.

Intuit projects the message that everyone's time is valuable and respected. Meetings are not held to satisfy protocol. They must serve a business purpose. The frequency and content of the meetings are directly related to work the team is involved in at any given time. The whole team decides how often to meet. Says Sillberg, "We identify (what is going on) at the meetings and ask, 'Do we need to meet three times a week?' On our team now, we have a stand-up meeting once a week and a team meeting once a week. And they are not about going through a laundry list about who is working on what. These meetings are focused on what is important at this moment. And those that are out of town call in so that the whole team is together."

Respectful practices ensure that Intuit employees are not afraid to express themselves in group meetings or one-on-one with their leader. Differences in perspectives and opinions are encouraged and solicited. "We do have heated discussions but we view them as fun," says Sillberg. "Employees can be really passionate about their topic, but they are not put down about it. We will talk about the data and the philosophy, but it is not mean. So then we have such great conversations. We can talk about the philosophical views around salary range and we get to what is the value to the employee. It gets into what is important."

As a result of the ongoing and open communication at Intuit, there is little need to address complaints of disrespectful behaviour. "On a day to day basis," says Sillberg "if two people are in disagreement, other than a business issue, they can go either to their boss or their HR business partner, or even a peer in their department.

It is not something that I see. I am sure conflicts exist but they get solved before they get to HR. My team does not see it. Most conflict gets generated at the emotional level; when you are dealing with people straight up, then that emotional stuff does not arise."

Respectful leadership requires a commitment to honest and open communication that is practiced across hierarchical lines. According to Sillberg, "We have really good debates. We do not all agree about what we need to do, certainly at the senior team level. It is always done respectfully. Even when we have really good debates we still all walk out together. Running this kind of business is not easy. It takes total commitment."

One critical part of respectful leadership is respectful recruitment and internal selection, which we looked at in Chapter Five. The second part is training. "We hire for attitude, then we train for skill," says Four Season's Ellen du Bellay.

Employers of Choice recognize the importance of ongoing training, including coaching and support, to produce the respectful leadership style they want. This produces the behaviour change required. "Once you have coached them, it just becomes the way they behave," says Sillberg. Training leaders to live the core value of respect ensures that respectful leadership becomes ingrained as a part of the culture.

Training for Respect

A number of years ago, I was delivering Respectful Workplace Training for managers in a large organization when a familiar-looking woman came into my session. I introduced myself and said I knew her from somewhere, but was embarrassed to admit I was not sure from where. She looked at me and said, "I was in this course a couple of months ago. I got a notice to attend today and so here I am." That surprised me. No one was supposed to attend these sessions more than once. I knew we'd be covering the same material and I was worried she might be bored. I told her if she wanted to go back to work, that would be fine with me. She replied that her firm had already arranged for her role to be covered that day, and it was a long drive back to her office, so she'd prefer to stay.

I noticed that throughout the day, this woman participated actively and asked lots of questions. I was pleased she did not seem bored. At the end of the day she told me that she was glad an administrative mistake had allowed her to attend the course a second time. "This is such a complex topic and there is so much to cover. I don't think I realized how much I missed the first time around. Having different people here also made a big difference in the discussions we had. I really got a lot out of today and I think I understand things a lot better now."

Usually I have no continuity with individuals in my training classes. I meet them once and then they go back to their workplaces. I have no way to reinforce my messages. What my training is doing, of course, is planting seeds. I encourage people to think about respectful behaviour and why we should be concerned about it at work. I help people think about their behaviour and the behaviour of co-workers. I challenge people to think about power, both their own and that of others in their workplaces. I even inspire and empower some of the participants to take action to speak up about disrespectful behaviour at work.

However, as we all know, if seeds are not cared for – if they are not watered, sheltered and weeded – they do not grow.

Employers of Choice understand the importance of hiring someone like me to train employees and encourage behaviours consistent with their desired culture. They also understand the need to nurture the seeds planted in a training session, which means follow-up. Training can be ongoing and reinforced in a variety of ways, especially through coaching. With that type of support, training produces the desired behavioural change.

In 1990, Ellen du Bellay was an employee at Regent Hotels in Australia. When Four Seasons Hotel Corporation bought the Regent Hotel chain that year, du Bellay experienced the Golden Rule culture for the first time, and almost immediately after the acquisition. She attended a training session on Basic Management

Skills and Conflict Resolution. To her surprise, the sessions were facilitated by Wolf Hengst, then president of Four Seasons Hotels Asia, and Meg Fisher, vice president of human resources for Asia. She soon learned that these senior executives spent a lot of time conducting training at Four Seasons locations.

You might ask why Four Seasons Hotels would let highly paid senior executives spend their valuable time training employees, when in-house trainers could do it for them. They would reply it ensures that the values of its Golden Rule culture become ingrained in every employee. Four Seasons believes that senior executives who have lived the culture are the best candidates to model the values to new employees.

"What became very clear to me," said du Bellay, who later became Four Seasons' vice president of learning and development, "was the power these executives had to transfer the culture – first by telling stories, and then by role modelling the behaviour every minute of every day they spent with us. It was different from any other training program I had ever experienced. I was impressed that people at such senior levels were willing to spend this much time on a few simple messages. I remember Meg Fisher, the HR president. She spent two days with me. She was able to be very clear about the philosophy."

Contrast that experience to one that a conference attendee recently reported to me. He had just started a new job that required him to attend a company course on workplace respect that had proven so disappointing, he'd decided to come to mine a few weeks later. The in-house session had been a one-hour lecture during which the facilitator had stated, "We have a respectful workplace here" before proceeding to dictate what the workplace rules were and what would happen to any employee who did not comply with these. And that was it. No discussion, no dialogue. What really struck him, he said, was how fundamentally disrespectful that approach was. He said that both he and his fellow employees had concluded that the training was just about the company meeting its legal obligations; it actually had nothing do with promoting respectful behaviour.

If you want to train employees to exhibit respectful behaviour, structure the training so it models that behaviour. The Four Seasons' training philosophy includes structured training, role modelling and mentoring. There's no "canned" training; it must be truly reflective of their culture. They understand that the training itself is one factor creating the respectful behaviour they want their employees to demonstrate.

Shortly after *Fortune* magazine comes out revealing Four Seasons' Employer of Choice status, the hotel executives get calls that start out like this: "My boss stays at Four Seasons and raves about your people, and so we want to know what training programs you do, and whether we can use them and get the same results here in this hospital… mortgage company… nursing home… hardware store…"

If it were that easy, of course, someone would have made the training into a pill and earned more money than selling hotel beds! They haven't, because it is not that easy. Four Seasons' training was forty years in the making. It started with Issy Sharp's simple philosophy, which influences everything from hiring to training to rewarding employees. As du Bellay says, "It's the length of service and sacrifices that these people make for the good of the guests, and it's the pride that they feel when the experiences they create mean something for someone, whether it be in Bali or Boston. None of that would be possible if we did not believe in the Golden Rule."

The Four Seasons Introductory Training Program is required of every new employee at every level. So a housekeeper may find herself sitting in the classroom with the new director of finance. That choice underscores the fundamentals of respectful leadership; employees are not segregated based on their hierarchical status. A new employee is a new employee, regardless of where they work or what their actual job will be.

Introductory training is required in order to ensure that employees of all stripes adopt the Golden Rule culture. Every subsequent experience is designed to reinforce that. An employer must be clear, consistent and rigorous both in hiring and in training for that culture. Culture building requires continuous commitment for the long haul. Each new employee has the ability to influence the culture.

The rigorous training program culminates in a stay in the hotel, during which participants talk about the culture and guests. Trainers use a lot of experiential exercises, as opposed to lectures, to communicate their message about how co-workers are to treat one another. This is more effective than exercises involving a lot of writing, given that most employees do not speak English as their first language. The company also uses Lego blocks to teach teamwork and marbles to teach communication. Trainers put marbles into foam batons, blindfold people and challenge them to catch the marbles, fill up the baton and empty it. The exercise emphasizes the importance of communicating with team members to avoid dropping marbles. A Trivial Pursuit-style board game called Create Your Own Hotel Company involves teams to drive home the same point.

The Four Seasons Introductory Training Program entails seven components staggered over a twelve-week period. Maslow's hierarchy of needs – a psychological theory about how basic needs must be met before a person can move on to other needs – guided the design of the training. The training emphasizes that the first order of business is to address the basic needs of safety, security and belonging, so that each employee will be able to really focus on her or his job. Four Seasons executives understand the critical relationship between their organizational culture and the experience of their guests. So when new employees come in on the first day, they're immediately made to feel expected and welcomed. Trainers review all their benefits and issue them their uniforms, etc., as if they were a guest.

Each new employee has senior executives involved in his or her introductory training. The first day concentrates on culture and incorporates storytelling. The general manager and hotel manager both tell stories, and the divisional heads conduct a tour. There are conversational exercises and drawing. The second day they start in their department, but the third day they return to the classroom. Once they have a context, trainers talk about the hotel's standards.

New employees each spend a day with their manager before being assigned a peer trainer, someone chosen on the basis of his or her job performance. The peer trainer works with the new employee for the next six weeks and receives a bonus when the employee they're mentoring passes a standards test, which indicates they know how to perform their job up to Four Seasons standards. After six weeks, employees return to the classroom for a training module that ultimately reviews core competencies and demonstrates how these competencies translate to behaviour.

After another six weeks of work, employees return to the classroom for training in intuitive service: "How to read a guest, anticipate needs, be intuitive about the needs of the guests and do that little bit extra."

It trains employees to think and take action independently so that their on-job behaviour truly reflects Golden Rule culture. They are expected to go beyond following rules and procedures, to live the core values by thinking about each individual guest and focusing on his or her needs. The Intuitive Service Module empowers employees to take whatever action they deem necessary to provide for the needs of the hotel guests.

After three months, employees know the basics of their jobs and have experienced the Golden Rule culture.

While the Intuitive Service module is trainees' last classroom portion of training, they still have one phase to go. Each new employee is invited to stay at their new workplace as a guest – not as a bonus or perk, but as a final phase of the training. The idea is that once employees understand their role in delivering the product – which is superior customer service – they should experience that product as the customer would.

This is yet another example of how this organization translates the Golden Rule into a living organizational culture. If they're expected to offer guests exceptional service, they need to know what it feels like to be a guest. Once they've experienced that, they're expected to voice any ideas of how they could improve the service. By then, of course, these new employees have developed relationships with many individuals across hierarchical lines, giving them ample resources and contacts to approach on that task.

An effective feedback loop, as we have stressed before, is critical to respectful leadership and common amongst Employers of Choice firms. Employees are trained to speak up, raise concerns and give feedback. And successful firms ensure that action follows such feedback.

When Four Seasons first introduced its Introductory Training Program back in 1992, one goal was to decrease the incidence of employees leaving within their first ninety days on the job. Initial results surprised executives: turnover actually increased. An investigation determined that employees in the largest department, housekeeping, were not being treated as well as other trainees. Given how the firm's reputation and promises raised housekeeping trainees' expectations, this set them up for double disappointment. Of course, the minute the study revealed the problem, the firm took measures to rectify it and retention improved. Annual turnover is currently seventeen percent compared with an industry average of thirty-six percent, no doubt as a result of the emphasis on culture.

By 1992, Four Seasons had been promoting and developing its Golden Rule culture for thirty years. That made the temporary glitch in housekeeping training stand out; it also presented the corporation with an opportunity. Four Seasons responded gracefully and effectively – all part of acting on the feedback loop.

Too often, I see companies that ignore such opportunities. I am called in to assist in figuring out what is going on after an employee opinion survey brings a problem to light, or after complaints have been filed. I generally find clear evidence of a host of disrespectful behaviours and associated culture problems, but meet with denial and resistance when I share that with the employer. This results in a lost opportunity for the organization, a failure to adapt and promote the change required for solid business results and enhanced organizational performance.

Sometimes I feel like I have unwillingly participated in a disrespectful practice. I am the one who has asked employees to share their concerns, under the pretext that I can get something done about it. And then nothing happens. I am inspired when I meet employees who have endured awful, ongoing disrespect at work but still believe that change is possible. It reaffirms my belief in the optimism of the human spirit, and I'm always pleased when their patience is rewarded, especially when I am part of that. Leaders are lucky when they have such committed and resilient employees. Perhaps it's those employees who will one day help them turn the firm around.

Management employees at every Four Seasons Hotel take 350 hours of training on topics like team building and conflict resolution. "It is all about what is expected of you as a manager – participative leadership, collaborative problem solving and respect for people as individuals," says du Bellay. Once again, the training is designed with the participants in mind. It is highly interactive, aimed at providing managers with the skills they need to lead and direct employees in a Golden Rule-style manner. Managers learn how to resolve their own conflicts and how to mediate through case studies. For example, one case study examines who should get priority using the service elevators in the morning. Both catering and housekeeping role-play with managers to establish a healthy communication model in which each party states their needs, asks the other their needs, and so on. A video helps teach managers how to mediate with an employee. It emphasizes how to get employees to state their needs, covers appropriate behaviour and builds in time for practicing situations.

Managers are supported in their learning the same way they are taught to support their direct reports. Trainers train managers to manage performance. Any managers who exhibit inappropriate behaviour may be assigned a mentor to assist them in understanding that their behaviour is unhelpful. The approach is not a punitive one, but a respectful and supportive one.

Executives at firms without these kinds of approaches often say they can't afford this level of training, particularly managerial training. They'll argue that it takes employees away from doing their jobs. Employers of Choice have the opposite perspective – that training all employees, and particularly leaders, is a business necessity.

Although we covered this in Chapter Six, here's a quick review of statistics that support this: Factoring in absenteeism, turnover, stress-induced illness, lost productivity and anxiety-related accidents, workplace bullying costs Canadian companies close to $20,000 per employee per year. Employees spend ten to fifty-two percent of their work time dealing with the effects of being bullied. One workplace bullying case ended in a $1.7 million settlement.

To ensure that they avoid such costs, the training philosophy of Employers of Choice includes ongoing support for each individual so that the goals of the training sessions are realized. At Intuit, managers must be able to handle the challenge of getting staff to embrace change. Intuit positions human resources personnel as business partners whose primary role is supporting leaders so that leaders can support their employees. HR staff serve as coaches as well as managers. They're expected to spend their time helping the leaders.

Supporting Success – Respectful Performance Management

Intuit understands the critical connection between a leader's behaviours and the working environment. Leaders are coached to communicate respectfully, particularly when dealing with job performance issues. Says Sillberg, "We want to make sure that our managers cannot abdicate their responsibility at all, even when they have a difficult conversation with an employee who is not performing. It is not a slap on the wrist. It is 'you are not doing well and what can I do to support you?' That is what creates a safe environment. That makes a huge difference in how people recognize their own shortcomings and growth opportunities. Then they are not afraid to say 'I have a problem.'"

Intuit recognizes the necessity of leading in a manner that

eliminates the fear that permeates so many of our workplaces. Fear often prevents leaders from taking action even when they find out there is a problem; they themselves are fearful that in disclosing there is a problem on their team, they will get that "slap on the wrist." It is that fear that encourages leaders to blame the employee rather than focus on what he or she may have done to contribute to the situation, and/or how to resolve it.

In a respectful workplace culture, asking for help is not considered a problem or viewed as a weakness. Asking for help is seen as a business practice that promotes organizational effectiveness and enhanced performance. Leaders know they can and should call on their HR business partner to help them. They appreciate that there is a shared goal: business success. They know they have a right to be supported to achieve that success. "If we have an extreme example of an employee who needs performance management, both the employee and the manager are supported in the process," says Sillberg of Intuit.

For me, this is not only a respectful way to do business, but a realistic and pragmatic one. Let's face it. No matter how great our training and coaching may be, performance issues will always arise. As we established in Chapter Three, building a respectful workplace culture means facing up to what is going on in your workplace, even when you don't really want to see it. As I often tell participants in conflict resolution sessions, avoidance is never a good strategy. Conflict is going to occur. The question is what to do when it does: choose to resolve it with respectful methods or pretend it isn't happening, avoid dealing with it and hope it goes away?

Performance management, like dealing with conflict, is not an activity that inspires people to jump eagerly out of bed in the morning. Most of us would prefer to delay dealing with it, or avoid it altogether. Matters rarely resolve themselves. The respectful thing to do is face what we have to face in a manner that makes it as pleasant and productive as possible. As I have learned with conflict resolution, when we get past apprehension to experience a positive outcome, we are more willing to try it again.

As Employers of Choice have learned, the key to successful performance management is to design a process that flows from the core organizational value of respect. This means delivering the information in a respectful manner. The leader should feel confident he or she can structure the conversation in a respectful manner that enhances relationships. It should be a dialogue about an issue both parties want to resolve. Employees should feel that despite the challenge, they are valued as an individual and the leader is interested in helping and supporting them. The message should be that it is okay to have challenges; we all have them. What is important is how we cope with them.

Intuit trainers emphasize that from the beginning, the employee must feel safe to engage in an open dialogue. Managers open with questions like, "So how did that go, and how could that be better?" Managers are trained to pay close attention not just to language, but to body language. That way, the person being coached feels less intimidated. "When you get feedback in a respectful, calm manner, you can think about it and reflect, and then you ask questions," says Sillberg. "We often don't recognize how we say something or the impact it has on others. By having someone help us to understand [that]…we can start to modify our behaviour."

At Intuit, respectful leadership means that leaders walk the talk when it comes to performance management. Every leader, including the CEO, is coached by an HR business partner. "I coach the executive levels. I coach my boss a lot and he is open to it. Recently he was providing coaching to a group of people. I reinforced how well he did based on the impact I could hear over the phone and from feedback I received as well."

Many of us regard performance management as negative because it happens only when something is wrong. Just like the news media reports mostly bad news, supervisors too often speak to employees about job performance only when there is a problem. They often engage in what is known as the feedback sandwich: insert constructive criticism between two positive comments. But beware: after experiencing this tactic a few times, employees soon see it coming and come to associate compliments with criticism.[2]

Employers of Choice don't fall into the trap because in these organizations, the emphasis is on ongoing dialogue between employees and leaders, not reactive measures triggered by an error or problematic behaviour. At SaskTel, for example, performance management training is conducted throughout the year, and concludes with an annual review. It is considered a critical part of achieving well-articulated annual goals of the corporate strategic plan. SaskTel explains the strategic plan, finalizes it with input from all departments, then delivers it to upper management, after which the company rolls it out. Each department develops its own plan for achieving the objectives, and each employee formulates his or her own individual plan. So at each year's start, all employees know their objectives and anticipate an end-of-year evaluation. "That is our goal," says Carolynne Warner, "that each employee can see how their performance is contributing to achieving organizational success."

This practice clearly demonstrates respectful leadership and tells employees they are valued. The system works best if employees get ongoing coaching and connection; leaders check in with them at least four times a year to see how they are progressing.

So, no need for the feedback sandwich; employees identify concerns about their own job performance and take action to address those concerns. "Part of our annual review is a development plan," explains Warner. "Each employee is supposed to consider what type of development they need. Managers and employee decide jointly what needs doing in order for that employee to develop in that area. It is partly career management and also about developing skills."

SaskTel employees choose from a variety of resources to develop their skills: formal training, a conference and books (SaskTel has a library of training videos). There's even an Excel spreadsheet on the intranet that walks employees through dealing with an irate customer.

Performance management at SaskTel is a truly collaborative process. As a result, it does not have the negative connotations that exist in so many organizations. SaskTel constantly evaluates and develops training to ensure an inclusive and responsive process. Ongoing support and training for employees that include leaders is "the way it is."

"Leadership training has had a number of phases. There are some programs for all managers. Everyone is strongly encouraged to take them. Right now the emphasis is on the five leadership characteristics: holding people accountable, resolving conflict, collaboration, valuing difference and innovation," says Warner.

After a minimum of six months in their position, new managers start the training, which they are to complete within eighteen months. The program covers change management, leading organizational change, crucial conversations, how to hold people accountable and how to deal with conflict and differences. Then there is a portion on innovation, after which they have to complete an assessment. These include a 360-degree assessment and two self assessments focused on thinking and learning styles, behavioural tendencies, personality traits and interests. Yet another portion introduces trainees to the five leadership characteristics and how they fit together. There is both group and individual training, and each manger receives written feedback and one-on-one coaching identifying strengths and areas in which they need to improve. The coaching also helps them look at the assessments and talk about why they received some of the feedback they did. Then there is also something called a Learning Café. It gives the individuals the opportunity to look at their own development and the tools leaders have to support them in developing their skills.

Because SaskTel is unionized, its leaders recognize the importance of training and supporting managers to work respectfully and collaboratively with union officials, including industrial relations management training – a required course for new managers and strongly recommended for all managers.

Seem like more than enough training to enable leaders to

manage with respect? Wrong. Yet another management training program is under development called Management Essentials. It will cover everything from performance management to attendance management.

Such ongoing evaluation and modification of training at Employers of Choice companies is directly related to an emphasis on availability, accessibility and accountability. Because senior leaders are constantly soliciting feedback, they can be and are respectful to employees' needs. And because they are respectful of those needs, they are also consistently responsive to those needs. Employees, regardless of where they sit on the organizational hierarchy, see that respect demonstrated and get the support they need to do their jobs comfortably and productively.

Jane Sillberg of Intuit has said, "Everyone wants to be better. Some people are bad because no one helps them get better. When you work for a high-performance organization, everyone wants to be good. It is like in the old days when you needed an extended family to raise a child. In our organization it is not a single person's job. We all support each other."

This perspective assumes the best about people. And when that is your framework, your interpretive lens, it cannot help but influence how you approach people. When you believe that everyone at all levels of the organization is interested in supporting you, you are willing and open to hearing everyone's feedback, knowing that their motivation is to help both you and the business succeed.

SaskTel, Four Seasons, KPMG and Intuit all use their employee surveys to collect very specific feedback on how leaders are doing. The results are used to formulate concrete action plans that every department is required to follow.

The survey is also seen as a training opportunity. Sillberg of Intuit puts it like this: "If we find that there is a problem (with a manager), we don't give them a slap on the wrist; we work with them. It is very public. Employees know the results for their department. Let's say we have a manager who has a rating of seventy-five percent when our goal is eighty-five percent. The employees have the opportunity to give feedback. They decide as a group how they want to proceed. If they decide they want to give feedback without the manager, they do that, and then the manager comes back into the meeting. There will be a spokesperson who will give the feedback. It is a case where the employees will help teach the manager. What I love about that is that you often have employees who have more experience than the manager, so why not allow them to do that, in a non-threatening way? It is a teaching experience. The managers are not threatened and they are not humiliated. Employees can have the HR business partner there, or they can go it alone. Our role is to facilitate the conversation. We help to facilitate the safety of that. That always connects back to the manager's professional development. If they need specific skills in change management, we find the support for them."

Employees "teaching" their managers. Managers who are learning from their employees. If that does not embody respectful, collaborative leadership, then I don't know what does. On the face of it, this goes against everything we are traditionally taught about those who hold positions of power. I mean, isn't the manager the one who is supposed to know what the employee doesn't know? I mean, isn't that why he or she is the manager in the first place? While many of us have grown up with those concepts, doing business today demands that we shift our perspectives and adopt a new paradigm, one that flows from an appreciation and a respect for individual differences and abilities without regard for hierarchy.

In a respectful workplace culture, leaders are prepared to learn from those they lead. Those they lead are not afraid to speak openly and honestly about their leaders or any other organizational issue. In a respectful workplace culture, leaders are open to hearing feedback about themselves and are willing to modify their behaviour and actions on the basis of that feedback. That willingness comes from the fact that leaders in a respectful culture feel fundamentally safe – to admit they have flaws, to admit they need help, to admit that an employee may know more than they do. It is the absence of fear that allows leaders to learn, grow and ultimately become better leaders. That's a win/win for leaders, those they lead and the organizations for which they work.

That absence of fear also promotes a leadership quality critical for business success in our multicultural workplaces. A fundamental of respectful leadership is a genuine interest and willingness on the part of a leader to get to know each and every individual he or she is leading. In a respectful workplace culture where fear is replaced by respect and curiosity, leaders are interested in discovering the unique skills, talents and abilities of every individual on their team. Understanding and embracing diversity is a required stop on the Road to Respect. And that is exactly where we are headed next as we continue our journey on the Path to Profit.

8

Respectful Management of Difference – Diversity, Discrimination and Dialogue

What motivated us is that it makes good business sense to provide a diverse environment for our customers. We want to mirror our community.

> —CLIFF YEO, advisor, human resources department, Canada Safeway Limited

IN THE MID 1990s, competition in the grocery business in the U.S. really started to heat up. On one end, big-box retailers like Wal-Mart and Target offered cut-rate pricing on grocery items. On the other end, up-market gourmet and organic grocers appealed to increasing numbers of health-conscious consumers. Leaders at Safeway started asking questions about their new business realities.

They wanted their company to prosper in an industry that already had very tight profit margins. They needed to develop a strategy that would ensure Safeway both survived the competitive onslaught and emerged as an Employer of Choice in the new millennium.

What struck those leaders most was the disparity between customers and their management team. Look around the next time you are in a grocery store. More than seventy percent of Safeway shoppers are female. Leaders at Safeway noticed that while their customer base was largely female, virtually all their supervisors and managers were male.

Culture evolves either by design or on its own. No one at Safeway had consciously decided that there was no room for women in management. Male leadership was simply the norm in the retail grocery industry. Leaders further noted that while there were lots of female employees working at Safeway, most did not progress into management. "When I took my first management training program in 1986, there were ten white males," recalls Cliff Yeo, human resources advisor at Canada Safeway. "We were clones: the same age, same demographic." Women tended to apply for cashier, deli or bakery work, but experience in the produce department was necessary to become a store manager. Women just didn't seem to want to work in produce. That was just "the way it was" at Safeway.

Safeway, aiming to become an Employer of Choice, chose to deliberately change its culture. Its strategy was to help non-traditional groups, particularly women, advance into management. To accomplish that, Safeway embarked on a formal diversity initiative in 1997. The firm's philosophy was "to do it right, not to be first on the block." In 2000, it launched the first piece of an overall diversity strategy, Championing Change for Women: An Integrated Strategy.[1]

Safeway realized that its diversity initiative would be successful only if all senior executives embraced the business case. So Safeway leaders pursued respectful leadership. The commitment came from the very top, from the CEO and corporate offices in the U.S. and Canada. Every member of the backstage team was required to attend a diversity seminar, as was every store manager, assistant, management trainee and department manager.

Ten years later, management trainees are no longer clones. The most recent management-training program's graduating class was composed equally of women and men and forty percent were visible minorities. In March 2006, just five years after introducing Championing Change for Women, Safeway received the Catalyst award, which recognizes companies with proven results in recruiting, developing and advancing women.

Interestingly enough, that same year another report gave Safeway's diversity initiative kudos. Lehman Brothers, the global investment bank, found that Safeway's diversity programs had led not only to substantial advancement for women and minorities at the stores and corporate office, but also to increased sales and earnings for the company overall. In an industry with razor-thin margins, Safeway is now a highly profitable $40 billion company with 200,000 employees throughout the United States and Canada. The report concluded that diversity is in fact good for business.[2]

This fact was not news to Safeway, least of all CEO Steve Burd. In his Catalyst award acceptance speech he stated that he felt odd getting the award because "all we did for the last six years is act in our own best self interest."[3]

The business case for diversity is based on rock-solid evidence. We are working in a global economy. We are living and working in truly multicultural environments. Embracing diversity makes good business sense.

Little wonder that businesses both in Canada and in the U.S. eagerly jump on the "diversity" bandwagon. Unfortunately, the majority have not replicated these results. Some find that their diversity initiatives create new conflict and tension. From experience, I know the reason is quite simple. Many corporate diversity initiatives, however well intentioned, are approached as "add-ons." Firms seek to superimpose them onto the existing culture rather than rethink and retool the dominant features of that culture. In this way, diversity is often forced on everyone, like a new but unpopular uniform. This approach is disrespectful to both existing employees and employees the firm hopes to attract. Rather than producing an inclusive and tolerant workplace, this approach promotes fear, prejudice and animosity between groups. It's doomed to failure. It's a journey that missed the on-ramp to the Road to Respect.

Diversity, Power and Disrespect

A number of years ago I was delivering Respectful Workplace Training to a group of municipal employees. We were talking about how human rights laws promote the recognition of differences and the balancing of rights. One participant commented that, in her opinion, the balance was getting skewed in the "wrong" direction. I hear this type of comment quite often. I asked her if she could share an example of what she meant.

She said she was really upset because the municipality had decided that employees could no longer say "Merry Christmas," as that might offend some clients. In the discussion that followed, it became obvious that this touched a nerve for a lot of people, regardless of ethnicity. As more employees joined the discussion, I heard anger expressed – at their employer, at fellow employees and at the clients responsible for the municipality's decision.

Why were these employees angry? Because anger is a secondary emotion that often masks anxiety, frustration or fear – and fear, as we have already discussed, is front and centre in issues like discrimination and harassment.

In imposing the "Happy Holidays" instead of "Merry Christmas" rule this municipality wanted to show respect to Canadians who don't celebrate Christmas. They wanted to recognize that their client base was changing. This is a good thing. Recognizing diversity is a business imperative in today's multicultural business environment.

However, in adopting a policy that said staff could no longer wish their clients "Merry Christmas," this employer inadvertently pushed the fear button. The employer's action caused employees to focus on their differences, and encouraged those differences to foster resentment and hatred. The new policy and the manner in which it was communicated fuelled employees' fears about changes taking place in their community and workplace. Those who celebrated Christmas interpreted the message as, "It's a new day. You are no longer as important. Now they are more important than you are."

This employer's message and approach were fundamentally disrespectful because they were neither consultative nor collaborative. There was no opportunity for feedback. No one seemed to have thought about how this change might affect employees. Some employees were angry because they felt the policy was unfair to them. Others were upset and/or angry as they were getting blamed for the new policy because of their race, religion or ethnicity. Within this latter group, many had never experienced discriminatory behaviour at work before. Their first taste of workplace prejudice was a result of a workplace policy allegedly trying to prevent prejudice! No one was happy about the decision. It was a typical command and control directive.

In short, this was a well-intentioned but poorly executed diversity initiative. The fact that hundreds more are made like this every day explains why nowadays the mere mention of diversity strikes fear into the hearts of employees of all stripes. White males in particular end up bracing for what they regard as a "blame and shame" game.[4]

American speaker and author Suzie Humphreys explains that fear is often the foundation of prejudice. "I had not been raised to be prejudiced. So how did I become one of the Americans gasping about racial blending? Fear, of course. Isn't that what's at the root of all hatred? Fear that someone else will take what's mine, or get my place in line, or take away my values and force theirs upon me or you."[5]

When you get right down to it, diversity is scary business. Much as we try and dress it up in politically correct language, diversity is about change: change that seems to involve challenging our very beliefs, lifestyles, values and power. It can be downright threatening.

The failure to recognize that fact can derail well-intentioned diversity initiatives. That is precisely what happened when that municipality imposed the no more "Merry Christmas" rule. Employees were angry because they felt threatened and disrespected. It wasn't simply the new rule; it was how it had been brought in.

In my experience, the application of human rights laws often unintentionally sow the conditions for conflict between groups. If women get jobs men used to get, if members of visible minorities get jobs white people used to get, it's easy to believe that some of us are now going to be losing out. First we can't say "Mer. Christmas," and the next thing we know, "they" will get extra paid days off for "their" holidays. Scary stuff. Diversity is a critical goal, but when we use disrespectful means to impose diversity, we have all the ingredients for the ultimate recipe of workplace disaster.

I often hear comments in my training sessions about reverse discrimination. The example cited is the RCMP and their hiring practices. This issue comes up because in 1986, Canada passed legislation requiring the RCMP and other federally regulated employers (banks, federal government service, inter-provincial transportation and telecommunications) to have an employee mix that reflected the general population in terms of gender and ethnicity. At the time, almost all RCMP officers were white and male. The RCMP had a lot of catching up to do in order to satisfy the new requirements.

Unfortunately, the legislation is similar to affirmative action legislation, a more controversial and earlier phenomenon that originated in the U.S. It's disliked for giving a substantial advantage to individuals based on race and gender. In Canada, legislators purposefully structured employment equity laws differently, but that difference was never clearly communicated within Canadian culture. The result of those laws was that many white men found themselves "disadvantaged" relative to other groups, most notably women and members of visible minorities, as hiring preference was given to groups that were under-represented.

When employment equity and the RCMP's history with it comes up in training sessions, someone always asks me, "Isn't that reverse discrimination?" Preferential hiring, "reverse discrimination," is perceived as unfair, not equal, and not giving everyone a chance. Everyone should get a fair and equal chance. Absolutely right, I tell my participants. That is exactly what human rights laws are all about. What we need to understand is why the legislation was enacted in the first place.

The reason was because not everyone was getting a fair chance. That was directly related to the dynamic of power. Our lawmakers looked at power in society and who had it. Power was concentrated within one group whose cultural practice was to hire according to the status quo. They concluded that unless those in positions of power were forced to change, those not getting a fair chance would in all likelihood never get one. Employment equity was seen as a way to "force" a change that would ensure everyone would get a fair and equal chance.

Interest in diversity springs from human rights laws, which are intended to promote respect and dignity for every human being. The law aims to empower us, in effect equalize us as individuals, so that each of us can realize our dreams. The goal is to give all individuals equal opportunity to realize their full potential in society. In theory, this is a concept that most of us can wholeheartedly support.

Until fairly recently, however, inequality has been the norm, the status quo in society. Author Kelly Nault writes, "Only a few decades ago, social norms were based upon inequality in which people commonly viewed others as unequal to themselves. The majority of the public accepted class distinctions based on race, socio-economics and gender as a way of life. White was better than black, dad was 'head' of the household, and children were to be 'seen and not heard!'"[6]

Human rights laws refer to those norms of inequality as discrimination, which they intend to eliminate. The Canadian Charter promotes a tolerant, fair, just and mutually respectful society – and workplace.

Given our society's entrenched inequality, we must have a carefully thought out strategy to achieve equality. Human rights laws form that strategy, and arose because traditionally equality has not existed. It has not existed due to power dynamics.

Our human rights framework is set up to address a historical power imbalance. Within this framework those with more power are the winners, those with less, the losers. In human rights the winners are the privileged who traditionally enjoyed access to power and opportunity – male Caucasians (whites). Historically, that applies to almost every profession, every job that bestowed power, prestige and privilege. Although twenty-five years of human rights laws have chipped away at that, it remains very much the case today.

If white men are the winners (referred to as "the traditionally advantaged group" in human rights speak), the losers (the "traditionally disadvantaged group" in Canada) includes women, members of visible minorities, persons with disabilities and aboriginals. Human rights laws are intended to empower these groups so that they can get a bigger slice of the power and privilege pie.

While I subscribe to the notion that we live in a truly abundant universe that has more than enough for everyone, most people do not embrace this philosophy. Our culture embraces the notion of scarcity, of a pie limited in size. As a result, many of us believe that more for you means less for me. If the traditionally disadvantaged groups will now get more rights, power and privilege, that must mean less left for the traditionally advantaged group.

This perspective creates a huge problem. The tendency to view matters as win/lose means that to some, human rights laws appear to be turning the traditional winners into losers. No one wants to be a loser. The traditional command and control, win/lose perspective encourages an "us versus them" attitude, where "they" are seen as the group threatening our lives, culture and traditions. These days, there seem to be more and more of "them" out there, and they do seem to be gaining ever more privileges. It can set fear meters soaring.

What we are trying to achieve is a society in which fair chance for everyone becomes the permanent reality. If we are going to be able to do that, we must accept our cultural history. People in positions of power have used that power in ways that have been unfair, disrespectful and downright cruel. They still do. Racism, prejudice and gender bias are woven into the fabric of human history. If we are going to be able to move forward and create a respectful and tolerant culture, we must be willing and able to acknowledge and accept that history. We must understand and appreciate how this history has impacted all of us, both in society at large and more specifically within our workplaces.

You know the old saying, we learn from our mistakes. And then there is the one about how when we fail to learn the lessons of history they tend to be repeated.

I am all for learning from our history, as long as our understanding of that history is accurate and unbiased. Many people within our culture exhibit disrespectful, power-based behaviours. To some extent, we are all victimized by our collective human history. While it is true that white men have traditionally held positions of power within Western culture, that does not mean that white men should be blamed for our history of discrimination and prejudice, or that they should now be made to "pay" for that historical reality by being disadvantaged or treated disrespectfully. It is not accurate, helpful or useful to label white men as the bad guys, the villains in the human rights story.

Unfortunately, however, our win/lose, us-and-them framework encourages this attitude. As I shared in Chapter Three, I have personally experienced how easy it is to buy into the us-and-them, good-guy/bad-guy myth. This negatively impacts the human rights framework that is supposed to produce a tolerant and mutually respectful society.

The reality is that you can't produce a tolerant and mutually respectful culture by forcing change on people. This is particularly true when the change seems to be about taking something away from them. No one will willingly embrace something that does not seem to be in their best interest. The win/lose, good-guy/bad-guy framework encourages fear, mistrust and prejudice. Rather than learning about respect, tolerance and inclusion, this approach is encouraging a divisive, us-and-them mentality. "They" want what we've got, and they are getting it because they have been victims. Now "we" are the victims and "they" are the villains. The fact is that no one is interested in working with the villains. People do not want to develop a relationship with someone they fear or feel threatened by.

Until we recognize and openly talk about our cultural history and the win/lose, us-and-them subtext, it will be very difficult for many of us to appreciate the crucial importance of human rights laws, and how those laws will result in a respectful culture that will benefit all of us. While there is no doubt that today's RCMP employee mix accurately reflects the diversity of Canadian society, the comments I repeatedly hear about reverse discrimination confirm that employment equity legislation, like that municipal "no more Merry Christmas" policy, unintentionally pushed the fear button. The unfortunate consequence has been increased anger, hostility and resentment toward both human rights laws and members of the traditionally disadvantaged groups.

When employers fail to recognize the us-and-them framework within their workplace culture, they risk embarking on initiatives to promote tolerance and respect that will rapidly encourage fear, anger and disrespect. As I said earlier, when we use disrespectful means to impose diversity to boot, we have all the ingredients for a workplace disaster. Too many employees are being told that like it or not, they have to be tolerant and respectful. Like kids at day care, they are told that they have to play nicely in the sandbox even when they really feel like throwing sand or kicking others out of the sandbox altogether.

When Chrysler Group's president and CEO, Tom La Sorda, said that he would "kick the ass" of any subordinates who failed to embrace diversity,[7] I came to two quick conclusions. First, that command and control, fear-based, disrespectful leadership is alive and well at Chrysler. And second, no diversity initiative at Chrysler will be successful until the culture is changed, top to bottom. Why? Because you can't bully people into being respectful. You can't order people to be tolerant. You also can't rob people of their traditions and then expect them to embrace threatening new traditions. Change has to be gradual, consultative and partially voluntary.

Remember my mention in Chapter Seven of companies wanting to superimpose Four Seasons' training programs without attempting to adapt them beforehand, without paving the way by changing their own culture first, and without even considering whether what worked for another company might be a successful fit? Such shortsightedness is a recipe for failure. There's no chance they'll produce the same results when imported wholesale and without regard for culture.

Four Seasons' respectful workplace culture was forty years in the making, and the firm's training programs work because they reflect that culture.

When Safeway wins an award or Lehman Brothers reports on firms profiting from diversity, it creates a buzz. Employers realize, on some level, that today's workforce needs an updated approach. Diversity is a relatively new issue. It has become an issue for us because our employee mix is very different than it was twenty-five, fifteen or even ten years ago. Given the reality of human history and culture, it is not realistic to expect all these different individuals to get along and work well together without some help. And you certainly can't force them to.

Diversity is about promoting respect and tolerance. It is about managing difference in an organization – difference often related to gender, race, sexual orientation, disability, age or other personal characteristics now protected in human rights legislation. Those differences are protected by law because traditionally, they have resulted in disadvantage. We refer to that disadvantage as discrimination.

Discrimination and its offshoot, discriminatory harassment, are fundamentally disrespectful behaviours. Diversity initiatives have arisen in response to them, as a means to address historical discrimination and create more accepting, tolerant relationships between individuals of different backgrounds. Diversity initiatives are supposed to promote respectful attitudes in order to fulfill the intention of human rights law. The goal is workplaces where everyone can truly enjoy equality of opportunity and outcome. Human rights laws and diversity initiatives are not about winners and losers.

When every employee who wants to succeed has the opportunity and support required, it's win/win for both the employees and the organization. A successful diversity strategy results in engaged, motivated and productive employees, but only after all levels of a firm engage in genuine dialogue about differences.

This is not easy to accomplish, particularly as discrimination and discriminatory harassment remain a reality of contemporary life. In many workplaces, yet another factor weighs in to the issue of a cultural mix: bullying and the fear it produces. The challenge is to manage difference to achieve a cohesive, unified and respectful workplace culture.

An organization wishing to reap the benefits that diversity offers needs to ensure that its approach is respectful to all employees. It should avoid the us-and-them, good-guy/bad-guy, command and control leadership trap. It must be clearly understood as a business imperative that will benefit everyone in the organization, white men included.

Employers of Choice understand that diversity is about recognizing and supporting differences in individual employees. It is about building relationships and trust between different employees and teams to produce a coherent whole – a new "us" that includes all employees. Respect for difference must be nurtured until it becomes embedded in the fabric of the organizational culture, until it becomes the "way it is."

Respecting the "I" to Create the "Us" – "Big D" and "Little d" Differences

According to Wikipedia, diversity means "the quality of being diverse, or different." Diversity can refer to multiculturalism – the ideology of including people of diverse cultural, religious, political and social backgrounds. It can also refer to diversity in business –

the business tactic that encourages diversity to better serve a varied customer base.

I believe that diversity as a business tactic must be the rationale behind any workplace diversity initiative. However, to realize that strategy, an organization must figure out how to incorporate an ideology of inclusion into its business model. It must determine how to encourage tolerance for difference among employees. There is only one way to make that happen, and that's to adopt respect as a core organizational value. When business practices are truly respectful, they are by definition inclusive and tolerant of differences in individuals.

One practical approach to managing workplace diversity is to distinguish between what I call "big D" and "little d" differences. "Big D" differences relate to group characteristics like gender, race or age, all of which are protected by law. "Little d" differences are individualistic – differences in work styles, communication styles and/or personal habits. While not as obvious as "big D" differences, "little d's" can contribute to a host of conflicts. Left to fester, these can mushroom into divisive problems that negatively affect individual and team productivity.

An effective diversity strategy has to incorporate an appreciation for both "big D" and "little d" differences to ensure a truly comprehensive and balanced perspective.

Fundamentally, of course, we are all different. We are all one-of-a-kind creations. Society, however, tends to categorize us from the moment we are born. If we are female, we get a pink blanket and frilly clothes; if we are male, we get a blue blanket and a tiny catcher's mitt. As we grow, we are differentiated by our ethnicity, religious traditions, sexual orientation and family status. We are constantly being asked to check this or that box so that we can be correctly categorized.

Our entire life's experience is affected by this categorization. We make assumptions, often subconsciously, about each other on the basis of which "boxes" we check. These assumptions and judgments are often formed as soon as we meet someone – male or female, white, black, brown, tall or short, fat or thin, able-bodied or not.

The external categories that society imposes on us affect us no matter where we work. There is always pressure to fit in, to be part of the group. When the dominant culture appears to reject you, it becomes pretty challenging to figure out how to fit in.

So, in many cases you don't try; you become part of one of the many subcultures organized on the basis of difference. These are by definition problematic for employers interested in a profitable and productive workplace; they go against fostering a sense of connection between employee and work team, employee and supervisor, employee and the organization as a whole. It dampens the sense of connection between employee and the organization's purpose, product and goals. Failure to appreciate how allowing subcultures to form affects relationship and connection can be a costly failure to employers in today's multicultural and diverse marketplace.

Every workplace has a distinctive culture. So before an employer tries making statements about promoting an inclusive culture, the firm needs a clear understanding of its current culture. If a dominant group is imposing its values on others, then the message employees take away is that they need to conform to the characteristics of that dominant group. Workplace culture needs to be both inclusive and cohesive for everyone to feel connected.

Some months ago I was contacted by a client interested in my services. I asked about the workplace and its structure, including its gender distribution. The client's response was very telling. "Like most workplaces, we have more women working in administrative positions and more men in management." The subtext: "This is the way it is," men with women in subordinate positions reporting to them.

I didn't ask this client to tell me why he thought there were more men in management. If I had, he might have said that women don't tend to apply for managerial positions, or that women seem uninterested in managerial jobs. Maybe he would have said women are not capable of being in management, or maybe he'd have pondered aloud whether there's a glass ceiling in business. He likely wouldn't have realized the truth: that the firm hadn't put much thought or effort into examining its culture.

Canadian women earn the majority of undergraduate and master's degrees and make up half of all Canadian workers. One third of Canadian managers are female, although few make it to the top corporate echelons. According to Catalyst's 2006 Canadian census of corporate board officers and top earners in the *Financial Post*'s top 500 corporations women make up only fifteen percent of corporate officer positions, only twelve percent of board directors and only 4.2 percent of CEOs. At this rate, it will take another five generations for women to comprise one quarter of corporate officer positions.[8]

That is not good news for Canadian women or Canadian corporations. Two Catalyst studies of Fortune 500 companies in the U.S. found that companies with more women at the senior corporate officer level outperformed those with fewer women by as much as thirty-six percent. Corporations with the highest female representation on their corporate boards delivered fifty-three percent more return on equity than companies with fewer women on their corporate boards. These studies concluded that corporations that fail to promote women into top echelons are falling behind in a marketplace where women influence eighty percent of all purchase decisions.[9]

While current workplace realities reflect historical prejudice, it is dangerous to assume that prejudice is still consciously being applied to maintain the status quo. Companies whose executives are intentionally withholding opportunities to women and minorities have a real problem that needs addressing. But in my experience, "intentional" discrimination is not the norm; it's just that the status quo is somewhat self-sustaining. Remember Safeway, where once executives decided to investigate, they found that the reason they had few female managers is that they were drawing managers from employees with experience in the produce department, where there was simply no tradition of women working?

Most of us find work based on the advice of friends and/or family, who by definition are "like us." Most of us, in fact, are most comfortable being around people who are "like us." I have a number of clients whose workplaces are dominated by one ethnic group. Why? Because they hire the bulk of their applicants from that same ethnic group. The good news is that their employees are sufficiently happy there to recommend the workplace to their friends. The bad news is that having one dominant group tends to encourage divisions and conflict for non-dominant-group employees.

Another fact I'd like to emphasize is that white men don't hold a monopoly on prejudice, discrimination and exclusion. Employees of many genders and races exhibit those behaviours, particularly when you throw power into the mix. That's why it's unhelpful to kick off discussions on diversity with an assumption that a lack of female or minority employees implies intolerance on the part of leaders. If we are interested in promoting tolerance, that must mean tolerance for everyone, including white men.

Diversity is about difference, and all businesses harbour differences. Managing these effectively rests on understanding and recognizing both "big D" and "little d" differences. We must start off with a curiosity about these and how they may be embedded into our workplace culture and reflected in our workplace practices. We must also avoid the "blame and shame" approach and be guided by our core value of respect.

Respectful Dialogue about Difference

Earlier, I mentioned a client who seemed to take in stride the fact that his workplace was dominated by male managers. If he'd said to me, "You know, I am starting to wonder why it is we have more men than women in management," I'd have suggested he and fellow leaders start a dialogue about that issue. Here are some questions he might have tabled with fellow executives:

Is our workplace culture dominated by one group, or by the traditions or standards of one group?

What types of differences, both "big D" (group differences) and "little d" (individual differences) do we have in our workplace, and how do these differences affect everyone's ability to fit in and feel included?

What messages does our workplace culture send about difference?

Does being "different" affect an employee's experience of our culture, and if so, at what levels, within the team, department and/or organizationally?

And finally, what would respectful appreciation and acceptance of difference look like? How can we promote commonality and connection to our values and our culture so that everyone feels part of the "us" that is our workplace community?

When KPMG embarked on its diversity initiative, executives started by asking questions both formally and informally. The formal questions were part of a survey, which can be a very effective tool for understanding how "big D" differences might be impacting your organization. A word of caution, however. Make sure you are prepared to take action on what the survey reveals. I have seen firsthand how a failure to take action after soliciting feedback from employees results in increased apathy, frustration and disengagement in a workplace. Employers of Choice ensure that employees see how their feedback directly shapes their own work experience, as well as the overall culture.

Prior to embarking on a survey process, clarify your business objectives. Why are you gathering the information? To find out how difference manifests in the workplace? If so, leaders need to be clear on why that is important, what that really means to them and how it may affect them and the organization.

KPMG used its survey results to launch a respectful and inclusive dialogue about how difference was manifesting in their organization. They took the time necessary to bring executives on board before disseminating the survey results to the rest of the organization. The dialogue was inclusive because the strategy was structured to allow everyone to participate. It was designed to ensure that everyone felt safe to voice an opinion.

They took a full year engaging in dialogue at the executive level so that everyone had enough time to really understand what the survey revealed. This allowed everyone to appreciate how the issue was affecting the business. They talked about the implications of taking and not taking action.

Rather than imposing a policy, KPMG broadened the dialogue after a year to include the next level of the organizational hierarchy. When those leaders had enough time to digest, understand and appreciate what the survey results meant, they became accountable for initiating dialogue with their direct reports, and so on down the organizational chart. Everyone in the organization had the opportunity to talk about diversity before any radical changes to practices or policies emerged. KPMG's communication and governance director Val Duffey says, "We talked to people about what we mean by diversity. There was a need to clarify what it was about and what it wasn't about. Once people understood and people started seeing what it was about, people started saying 'that makes sense, I get it. I see why we need this education and awareness.'"

Getting all employees to understand and buy into the "why" of diversity is critical in ensuring that a diversity strategy results in respectful management of difference. When a diversity strategy flows from the core organizational value of respect, dialogue becomes the foundation of the process. Truly respectful dialogue must be structured sensitively and inclusively. Leaders need to think about how they can create a safe place for people to express themselves about matters not usually discussed. They need to address the fear that often prevents employees from talking about differences.

When it comes to "big D" differences, information gathering (including surveys) can provide the type of information required for leaders to determine if systemic practices are disadvantaging individuals of minority race, gender or sexual orientation. Most workplaces don't harbour glaring examples of intolerance and prejudice. In my experience, "big D" differences are more subtle. Micro-inequalities are organizational or departmental practices that stem from our assumptions about people different than us. They are often embedded in the way we do things in our organizations.

It is the subtle messages that people absorb and resent: "It's okay to be different as long as you are not too different. It's okay to be gay; just don't talk about it too much or be too obvious about your sexuality. It's okay to be Muslim; just don't let anyone see you praying anywhere." Of course, no one makes these comments overtly. They're just messages that members of "other" communities pick up on. And they add up to the message that a dominant group exists, and everyone needs to try to align themselves with this group's values and characteristics.

Early on in this book, we discussed the aboriginal corrections department employee who didn't look aboriginal, but experienced discrimination once he pointed it out. Co-workers basically implied that it was okay for him to be aboriginal as long as he was willing to participate in the behaviours considered "normal" at the Metro Toronto East Detention Centre. His problems started when he objected to and tried to change those norms, which involved overt racist comments. When employees observe what happens to someone like that man, they decide they're being told to "put up and shut up." The pressure to fit in, the fear about what might happen if we make it known that we don't, discourages us from engaging in dialogue with our co-workers or leaders about our differences.

I have been presenting Respectful Workplace Training for years, my main goal being to use these to start a dialogue about respect at work. I often start my sessions by asking participants if they think we can train people to be respectful. I hear lots of opinions on that!

I discuss this with participants to emphasize that while we can talk about respectful behaviour, create expectations about demonstrating respectful behaviour and hold individuals accountable for doing so, ultimately, being respectful is a choice each individual makes.

It is in our best interest to make that choice because it results in a better work experience. Disrespectful behaviour causes unhappiness, conflict, loss of focus and productivity, and often physical or emotional illness. Too often, however, we accept or fail to recognize disrespectful practices. We don't realize it's disrespectful to ignore something bothering us at work – disrespectful not only to ourselves, but to our co-workers.

I structure my training sessions to encourage dialogue about difficult issues seldom spoken about openly. Both in the sessions and in subsequent conversations with the employer, I stress the importance of keeping that dialogue going after the training. Culture change is an ongoing process.

Dialogue and diversity are two sides of the same coin. The challenge is finding a way to encourage dialogue about workplace difference.

As I've said, fear-based workplace practices like bullying and harassment effectively muzzle employees. If an employee survey reveals the presence of these practices, employers need to tackle them before they can tackle diversity. To use a farming analogy, you have to till the soil before you plant anything or the harvest will wither and die.

Diversity training, an important component of any diversity strategy, can be a great way to begin the dialogue. Due to the sensitive and controversial nature of the subject matter, the training must be relevant to the workplace, must promote dialogue and understanding about the issue and must be facilitated in a respectful manner.

When Safeway introduced diversity training for leaders it avoided imported, canned training, instead designing a course relevant for the realities of its workplace. One of the main goals was to get leaders talking. One issue they talk about is supervising employees whose first language is not English, a particularly challenging aspect of managing difference.

When I first started consulting and writing Respectful Workplace policies, employers would ask me if they could "make" their employees speak English. Well, I advised, employers can do anything they want in the workplace as long as a law or collective agreement doesn't forbid it. And English is the language of work in British Columbia, so employees should speak English when they are working. When they are on a break they can speak any language they want. This was ten years ago, and at the time, it did not occur to me that this was not a respectful way to approach the situation or manage employees.

Then one of the employers who adopted my recommended English-language policy called me some years later. He needed help dealing with the workplace conflict that had resulted from that policy. What can I say? We learned, and happily, the client has hired me many times since, with happy results.

To help that client, I conducted focus groups to see what the problems were. We discovered that employees whose first language was not English felt that the policy was discriminatory. They felt singled out and picked on. Those whose first language was English said it wasn't helping anything, as everyone spoke their own language until they saw a supervisor or manager coming. They even did so purposefully, some felt, because they were angry with the policy. The supervisors said that trying to "catch" employees made them feel like police. As for the few employees who got caught and in some cases disciplined, everyone regarded them as unfairly victimized. This made it clear to me that the policy had to be scrapped.

We also learned that the choice of language was causing some serious inter-personal problems. This was a manufacturing environment where employees spent their shift chatting with co-workers. The employer had no problem with that, as long as the conversation did not interfere with the operation, which for the most part it did not. The problem was that employees were bidding on shifts so that they could work with friends who spoke their language of origin. Inevitably, on some shifts those who could not speak the dominant language felt isolated and excluded. Some felt lumped in with employees based on what language they spoke. Some ended up having no one to talk to at all. And some really wanted to join in with the joking and laughter, but the language barrier prevented that. There were also employees who feared they were being talked about when co-workers looked at them while speaking in a language they could not understand.

I have found myself in the latter situation on numerous occasions. Years ago, I was acting as a negotiator in collective bargaining for a client whose employees all spoke English as a second language. Everyone on the bargaining committee except the union negotiator and I spoke Punjabi. I noticed that when the union negotiator was in the room, the employees spoke English. However, when I was alone, on breaks or returning early after lunch, everyone spoke Punjabi. It was as if I wasn't there. I mentioned this to them a couple of times, but it made no difference. After a while, I took to waiting outside until the union negotiator arrived.

I understood that we were in an acrimonious process that may have contributed to the behaviour, and that most of the employees did not have a good command of English; it was an effort for them to speak it. But it made me uncomfortable, and I had communicated that to them, so I had to wonder: Did they not realize they continued to speak their own language even after I asked them not to? Did they not care about what I wanted or how I felt? It did not feel respectful to me. It gave me insight into how the situation must feel for those who experience it on a day to day basis.

It also made me realize the importance of dealing with the language issue at work, and how much language affects our workplace relationships. When we do not communicate regularly with co-workers, it severely hampers our ability to pursue meaningful relationships. Let's face it. It is hard enough to understand each other and get along when we do speak the same language. We really can't engage in a dialogue about difference if we literally don't speak the same language!

Language in the workplace is one aspect of managing difference we need to talk about. Employers need to ask themselves whether the firm's work requires employees to have a bit of English, a working knowledge of English, or a real command of both verbal and written English. It may even make it desirable to actively recruit multilingual employees. Safeway's customer base is very diverse, and that diversity varies by store location. Having multilingual employees is a real business asset for Safeway. The issue is how to ensure that having multilingual employees does not cause divisiveness and subcultures. Leaders have to develop a respectful strategy to manage this difference, one specific to the particular workplace.

Safeway expects employees to be able to speak English, but does not require them to speak it at work. "We don't tell people they can't speak their language of origin," says Cliff Yeo. "The only time we would have an objection is when it impedes our operation." And yet, Safeway has made it clear that it expects employees to be mindful and respectful of who is around. "We have found that when they are at lunch, they may be speaking their language of origin and unaware that it may be bothering someone. If someone finds it offensive, the manager just speaks with them. Out of 11,000 employees, we have an issue maybe once or twice a year. [Then] we don't hear about it again."

The reason leaders at Safeway don't hear about it again is their respectful workplace culture. Employees are encouraged to raise issues when they occur. When they raise an issue with a manager, the manager knows he or she is accountable for dealing with it, and takes appropriate and respectful action. Finally, the individuals who inadvertently offended are prepared to modify their behaviour due to the feedback they get. Why? Because at Safeway, the cultural norm is a respect for difference and accountability for demonstrating that respect.

Engaging in dialogue about language at Safeway has resulted in the development of a buddy system for new employees whose first language is not English. It's called the new employee alliance. It pairs the new employee with an employee that speaks their language of origin.

Let's think about why the "new employee alliance" demonstrates respect. First, it sends a clear message that being different is okay and that a person can manifest that difference openly at work. It recognizes the potential training difficulties that an employee whose first language is not English may experience, as well as the fact that it may be difficult to have to speak a language that is not one's first language all day when at work. That demonstrates empathy. It supports that employee by providing the opportunity for familiarity and assistance. It says, "We want you to succeed, and here's something we can do to help you succeed."

And it develops relationships. It is the relationships we have at work that connect us to our workplace. Disrespectful behaviour can damage and destroy relationships. Building relationships is one important goal of respectful leadership. The more relationships we have at work, the more connected we will be to our workplace. And when those relationships connect us with others outside our own team, we promote a sense of connectedness to the greater whole, the "us" that is our entire employee group.

While language is a "big D" difference, the buddy approach also recognizes and respects "little d" differences. When the buddy option is offered, each employee can decide if and when he or she needs to access it. Ultimately, the goal of a diversity initiative must be to differentiate and appreciate each individual as unique, regardless of the "big D" group with which someone might identify. That practice, which flows from the core corporate value of respect, then translates into a behaviour that forms part of the workplace culture. Being appreciative and respectful of difference becomes the "way it is" in that workplace.

Consistent with practices at other Employers of Choice, most management employees at Safeway come up through the ranks. The challenge for Safeway leaders was to find a way to change the historical practice that resulted in male leadership in the grocery business. They had to look at leadership practices and messages, both overt and covert, that were part of their corporate culture to determine what needed to change and how to engineer those changes.

Publicly adopting a program like Championing Change for Women certainly is a great way to let female employees know that the company wants to create more opportunities for them in management. However, a critical part of making a program like that successful is actively encouraging potential future leaders to start thinking of themselves as such, and then to support them in that quest. That happens through dialogue.

Dialogue develops relationship. A critical aspect of respectful leadership is the development of relationship between a leader and his/her team. As we discussed in Chapter Seven, a respectful relationship includes ongoing dialogue rather than annual performance management meetings. Ongoing dialogue and the relationship that results from it ensures that employees feel comfortable talking about career aspirations with their leader. It also allows a leader to really get to know direct reports.

At Safeway, managing difference involves appreciating the fact that ethnicity and gender may unnecessarily influence an individual to perceive career path limitations. In other words, management may need to give that person extra encouragement.

To ensure that leaders approach employees, Safeway has included mentoring as a critical component of both its leadership development program and its diversity strategy. Every Safeway manager, including the Canadian and U.S. CEOs, mentor a number of employees – direct reports and employees from other departments.

Mentoring builds relationship and enhances connectivity. "Part of our diversity initiative is our mentoring initiative. It has evolved like crazy," says Cliff Yeo. Typically the mentor is a store manager and the mentee a manager trainee. The program's purpose is to steer employees into the management training program. A development program is created for each employee. The mentor meets with the employee every two weeks to assist them in acquiring the knowledge, experience and skills they need to progress. As Safeway employees are members of a union, the mentoring program has been negotiated with the union and forms part of the collective agreement.

This approach allows Safeway to profile each mentee to see where they are at and where they need to be. That helps women in the grocery industry because it allows mentors to pinpoint what knowledge they need to acquire, and place them accordingly.

According to Cliff Yeo, "Now that we have more female managers, other women think 'I can do that.'"

Respecting the "Whole Person"

Another reason more women at Safeway are starting to think they can pursue leadership positions is Safeway's focus on work/life balance and scheduling flexibility. These are integral components of Safeway's diversity initiative. When leaders at Safeway analyzed the standard route for leaders and the unspoken cultural practices, they found a number of practices preventing women and others from considering management a viable career option. One was the need to relocate to gain experience as one moved up the corporate ladder. Saying no to relocation was traditionally considered a "career limiting move" at Safeway.

In human rights lingo, we refer to this as adverse effect discrimination: a law or practice that is not overtly discriminatory but has a negative effect on one particular group of people. Such practices remain unidentified problems or obstacles embedded in workplace culture unless leaders make a conscious decision to examine them.

Travelling was part of my job when I worked at the airline. When I first started, it was a perk I relished, particularly after I started to travel business class. Let me tell you, it is hard to be happy sitting behind the curtain when you have experienced what it is like up front!

Becoming a mom changed my interest in travelling. When my boss first offered me the human rights advisor position, she stressed that it would not involve the same level of travelling my labour work had. As a mother herself, she understood before I did that travelling was going to take on a new perspective for me.

No travel was required of me in that new position until my reporting relationship changed. I will never forget the day my new director called me in and handed me a file on a harassment complaint in one of our northern bases where there were no trained internal investigators. He wanted me to leave that afternoon to start the investigation.

Panic formed in the pit of my stomach. There was no way I could leave that afternoon. I was still breastfeeding my daughter; she had yet to accept a bottle. I looked up and told him I could not go and explained why. I told him I'd find someone else. His frown held no hint of sympathy; I knew immediately that I'd just made a "career limiting" move.

Anger welled up inside me. Oh, all well and good for him, I thought, with his stay-at-home wife. He could pick up and go at the drop of a hat. Of course, he said nothing overt about how this would affect my career. And I found a team to take my intended place that day. However, I knew my days at the airline were numbered. If travelling wherever and whenever was a requirement for moving up in that company, it didn't matter whether the law required my employer to accommodate me. I had made my priorities clear. I had put the needs of my family first. I had gone against the grain of the prevailing corporate culture. I had clearly indicated I didn't "fit."

Laree Renda has been with Safeway for more than thirty years. Now the executive vice president and chief strategist and administrative officer of the U.S. division, she started her career as a part-time bagger when she was sixteen. In the early 1990s she made what she thought would be a career limiting move; she refused a promotion that required relocation. She and her husband were not prepared to move their three children from their local Catholic school. But her refusal coincided with the arrival of U.S. CEO Steve Burd, a leader instrumental in introducing Safeway's corporate diversity initiative. He offered her another opportunity that would not entail moving: vice president of corporate retail operations. Renda has progressed through the ranks ever since, despite continued refusals to uproot her family. She has also repeatedly been named one of the fifty most influential women in business by *Fortune* magazine.[10]

Renda believes she has been fortunate to work for individuals and later a company that respected her need to put her family first. However, she also says, "I have never been afraid to raise my hand and say 'this is important,' when my children needed me."[11]

My experience is that most employees are not as bold as Renda, typically due to the unspoken norms of the workplace culture.

Without dialogue and relationship, how is a leader to know what employees need to remain interested in working for the company? Without dialogue and relationship, leaders risk losing talented employees in whom they've invested time and money. To demonstrate a commitment to managing difference, executives have to be clear and consistent in delivering their message, demonstrating respectful leadership and relationship building. Employers of Choice know what they need to do to support and empower employees.

Scott Gibney, public affairs manager at Canada Safeway, had personal experience with leaders demonstrating a commitment to work/life balance when his partner was about to give birth. "When her water broke ahead of schedule, my VP came into my office and said, 'You go! You don't answer those emails.' He threatened to call security if I didn't go."

Walking the talk in managing difference means you have to consider both big and little D differences. "We try to recognize work/life balance," says Cliff Yeo. "We do that for everyone. Rather than a fixed schedule, we allow the district manager to be flexible. If you have to be at your child's hockey game, we will make sure you can be. A lot of our jobs are with students, and we work around their exam schedule." To ensure that management can offer that type of flexibility to each employee, Safeway has negotiated the practice into the collective agreement.

As we have discussed, a genuine diversity initiative must incorporate the core value of respect for differences. It is about respect for each individual as well as the group. It is not about assuming women will need flexibility because they are women, while men won't because they are men. Such assumptions are what prejudice and discrimination are all about.

It is also not about making exceptions to the rule. It is about changing the rule, challenging assumptions, creating a culture that makes it safe for individuals to be themselves. We do that by incorporating respectful practices.

These days many employees, both women and men, want to work in an organization that promotes work/life balance. For some that interest flows from being a working parent. For Dianne Lamendola, Safeway's group vice president for information technology, that desire for flexibility flows not from motherhood, as she has no children, but from the athletic pursuits and charitable activities in which she is so heavily involved. Those activities are important to her, and her employer's willingness to recognize that instills a high degree of commitment in her.

Lamendola endeavours to excel at her very demanding job. She values the fact that her employer respects her and provides her with the flexibility to leave early or arrive late for her commitments outside the office.[12] That flexibility, which flows from Safeway's diversity initiative, is a major factor in Lamendola's choice to remain employed there. She gets to do a job she loves as well as have a lifestyle she wants. Safeway gets a committed leader who acts as a role model and mentor for a host of other Safeway employees – a true win/win outcome.

When I first called to interview KPMG's Val Duffey, she started off by apologizing that she was going to have to cut the interview short because she was a single mom with a baby at home, and the nanny had just called to tell her the baby was sick. She was leaving work early to be with her son.

KPMG promotes work/life balance as an important component of its diversity strategy. Duffey told me it is standard practice for the company to make sure that individuals are set up with the technical support they need so that they can work from home outside of core hours if they need to.

KPMG does so because it makes good business sense. It allows the firm to attract and retain empowered, loyal and committed employees. "In terms of being a single mom," says Duffey, "I can't imagine working for any employer but KPMG. From my boss to my team to my internal clients, everyone is incredibly supportive. My hours are flexible. I use my breast pump during my work day, and on days like today, when I need to leave work, no one bats an eyelash."

Employees at Intuit enjoy the same type of flexibility. As an organization with a high performance culture, Intuit often requires employees to put in long hours. However, Intuit tells them this should not negatively impact their personal or family life. At Intuit, managing difference means ensuring that when employees are at work, they are focused on their work and not distracted by issues that may need their attention outside of work.

Says Jane Sillberg, HR director at Intuit, "In the '70s and '80s, I often heard 'leave your personal life at the door.' That makes no sense to me. Intuit doesn't just tolerate personal lives; we embrace them. We have high chairs and booster seats in our lunchroom. We invite the families to use the fitness facility. Work is way bigger than the individual. If an employee has a sick child, we let them do what they need to do. If your child gets sick in the middle of the day, what can you do? We don't worry about which day off they access. We say, 'How can we help?' People know what they need to do. They don't need to be watched. We want them to deal with the situation and come back to work comfortable that they can be there. If they have to work a lot of overtime, we suggest they send their partner flowers, or send in a pizza for dinner. No one abuses it. If they do, we deal with it."

A Foundation of Trust

You start from a place of trust and show respect by demonstrating that trust. You are being respectful when you provide flexibility and support for employees as they need it. You empower employees to do what they need to do so that they can be fully present and engaged when at work. You manage respectfully by staying involved and building relationship. As a result of that involvement, you can take action when someone's behaviour is not consistent with corporate values.

Some firms take the approach, "We can't do that because people may take advantage of that practice or benefit." That philosophy arises from a disrespectful culture. It flows from the command and control perspective, the days of assembly-line production. It flows from the belief that people are really lazy and must be made to work hard. It's disrespectful and highly inaccurate to assume that, left to their own devices, most people will sit around and take advantage of any opportunity not to work.

Communication and trust are intricately connected. I can't even begin to count the times I have seen communication failures in organizations. In effect, every conflict at work results from ineffective, problematic, disrespectful or the complete absence of communication. If we are interested in building trust within our organizations, our workplace culture must promote ongoing and respectful communication, which by definition includes respectful dialogue.

Clear and respectful communication is particularly important when an organization is introducing changes of policy or practices – especially when those changes are connected with managing difference at work. When I am delivering human rights training, I frequently hear about how standards have dropped due to the integration of women, members of visible minorities or individuals with disabilities into the workplace. The underlying message is that it is easier for them than for "us," that "they" are getting a break we didn't get, benefits or opportunities we don't have. When that perception is out there, we need to talk about it. Everyone must understand what changes to traditional practices are really about. Yes, change has taken place. But just because standards are different does not mean they are less demanding or inferior. They are just different, and the reason for the difference is to allow more individuals, different individuals, to succeed.

Safeway asked questions about their traditional cultural practices. Safeway execs were interested in determining whether modifying those practices would lead to a more diversified leadership. They asked themselves if there was a way for employees who couldn't easily relocate to obtain the skills they needed to be promoted. The executives' determination to be more open-minded and to ask such questions resulted in Safeway's Retail Leadership Development program. Today, relocation is no longer required of individuals interested in management at Safeway, and leadership has diversified.

The Retail Leadership Development programs not only identify what skills and development each leadership-track employee requires, but supports them by paying up to eighty percent of their education and tuition fees. This practice builds connection and loyalty to the organization. It is a respectful way to build trust through the management of difference.

Employee networks are another vehicle through which Employers of Choice achieve these goals. While networks involve both peer support and mentorship, they differ from traditional mentorship.

A network is a group of employees who come together based on a "big D" difference such as gender, ethnicity, sexual orientation or disability. It is an employer-supported, employee-driven initiative. Safeway's first network was for women. "The whole purpose is for women to support and mentor each other," says Cliff Yeo. The women's network brings in speakers both from within and outside the organization, four times a year, usually over the lunch hour. Employees interested in attending work it out with their store manager. Sometimes the network meetings go on the road to ensure that employees in far-flung locations can take part.

So far the women's network is the only one operating at Safeway in Canada. Other groups have not shown an interest in starting one. But in the U.S., Safeway has networks for African Americans, Asians, Hispanics and lesbian, gay, bisexual and transgendered employees. None of these networks are exclusive to the dominant group; anyone is welcome to participate. (Men who participate in the women's network often help advise them on career moves.) In this way, these networks become an informal way to raise awareness and share information about difference within an organization.

At Intuit Canada, the newest network embraces recent graduates, whom the firm found were arriving with a need for more skills in socializing. Intuit supports its networks by allowing meetings on company time and sometimes providing funds for events. Like at Safeway, all of Intuit's networks are welcoming to all employees.

The networks help the company understand its employees and their cultures.

Networks are also a feature of diversity management at both KPMG and SaskTel. At KPMG, the women's network was the first. In its PRIDE network for gay, bisexual, lesbian and transgendered employees, individuals can participate anonymously or visibly. According to Val Duffey, PRIDE involved a big shift for the firm. But she was pleased when recently an openly gay diversity champion told her that where few gays were open about it five years ago, it's now possible to be openly gay, feel supported and pursue career success.

KPMG also has a working parent's network, which meets both in person and virtually via technology. Even before KPMG adopted its formal diversity strategy, the culture allowed for formal flex work, including part-time, reduced work hours, a compressed work week and a gradual return after maternity leave.

"While work/life balance is part of our culture," Duffey notes, "that doesn't mean people don't struggle with how to do it. That is what the network is about, sharing personal strategies around how to work with your peers, balance your absences, work with clients and your boss."

The newest KPMG network formed as an offshoot of the working parents' network. It is a network of employees with special needs children. This is a great example of how parameters expand when we start to think about respecting difference at work. "When people feel valued and engaged, the time that they spend at their desk is productive time," says Duffey.

Networks at SaskTel aim to provide both employee support and a bridge into the community the organization serves. The firm lets employees know that it has a framework for networks and will assist anyone who comes forward with an idea for a network. Its youth network draws on employee volunteers as well as volunteers from local high schools. The group works with youth on community projects.

Among SaskTel employee networks are SAEN, SaskTel Aboriginal

Employees Network, and SEND, SaskTel Employee Network on Disabilities. These groups participate in community events on a volunteer basis.

Networks provide a safe place to talk about difference, invite curiosity and promote learning and awareness about difference. They build relationship across organizational power lines and beyond team and departmental boundaries. They offer opportunities for sharing and support, provide a vehicle for problem solving and build trust and loyalty.

If You Build a Respectful Culture, They Will Come – Attracting and Retaining a Diverse Workforce

The SEND network at SaskTel reflects one of the newest aspects of diversity management – managing issues related to individuals with disabilities. Historically, in the 1970s and '80s, workplace human rights complaints were dominated by sex discrimination. Then it was race discrimination. Now it is discrimination against those with mental or physical disabilities.

In Chapter Six we looked at the case of Mr. Keays, who was fired from his job at Honda and subsequently developed post traumatic stress disorder. An obscene amount of money has been spent as this case has wound its way up to the Supreme Court to try and determine who did what to whom. In my mind there is really no winner in these types of court proceedings. Both Mr. Keays and Honda have suffered in this adversarial and acrimonious process, an outcome that would have been avoided if the workplace culture at Honda was one characterized by respectful dialogue about difference.

One critical aspect of managing difference of individuals with disabilities relates to how employers deal with and accommodate workers who, like Mr. Keays, become injured or disabled in the course of their employment. To avoid costly court proceedings as well as the loss of valuable employees, organizations must adopt a truly respectful and flexible process to manage those cases, one characterized by collaboration and dialogue.

Too often the focus is on what the individual can't do, as opposed to what that person can do. Individuals with disabilities have much to offer in terms of knowledge and skills. The respectful approach is to focus on the ability rather than the disability.

As talent pools shrink, some employers are discovering a relatively untapped goldmine of talent. In British Columbia, there are an estimated 300,000 people of working age who have disabilities – two-thirds of them not in the workforce even through they want to be. Of these, approximately 34,000 have college diplomas, 30,000 have trade certificates and 28,000 have university degrees.[13]

Surely, inaccurate assumptions about these individuals' capabilities contribute to that high underemployment. If we are interested in accessing this labour pool, we must suspend those assumptions and become curious about individuals with disabilities. We must develop a strategy to attract them into our workplaces. We can't wait for them to come to us. Employers must take proactive steps to send a clear message that the workplace is one with opportunities for individuals in non-traditional categories like this.

A number of years ago I was working with a municipal employer in a region that had experienced huge changes in its constituents' demographics. The municipality was interested in ensuring that its employee population reflected the new mix. Try as it might, however, it found that individuals from non-traditional groups were not applying for jobs in certain departments. My client and I started asking questions and speaking to community leaders. That's when members of those communities told us they thought the municipality was not welcoming to them.

It is hard to know how such an impression formed. Maybe it was a result of one individual's bad experience, maybe more than one. Or maybe the community made assumptions. Whatever the reason, the fact is that an employer can't have diversity until individuals from "different" communities perceive that they will "fit" into its culture.

So the first order of business is to ensure that a workplace is welcoming. The next task is to send a clear message to those individuals; to let them know the workplace is interested in employing them.

The problem is, unless a firm is hiring under employment equity legislation, it can't "discriminate" in its advertisements. It cannot state a preference for "non-traditional" groups. To attract such groups, one has to seek them out, engage them in dialogue, form relationships with them and invite them to consider employment.

Says Safeway's Cliff Yeo, "We actively reach out into the community. It really is for the greater good because the more other employers see our success story, the more it will encourage them to [adopt diversity strategies]."

Safeway uses the same approach to encourage individuals with disabilities to apply as they do with any other group. They go and talk to them. They form relationships with organizations like the BC Association for Community Living. Safeway actively recruits individuals with developmental disabilities, and currently has around 100 developmentally disabled employees.

Safeway hired a high school graduate from a school of the deaf who initially helped in the meat department, but soon developed a goal to be a meat cutter. "Now that is what he does. He is a very charismatic young man," says Yeo.

Another success story is in Duncan, BC, where a store remodelling required managers to hire roughly fifty new people. Since the store is on reserve land, Safeway saw it as an opportunity to change the makeup of their staff. They went to the aboriginal community, explained what kind of people they were looking for and asked reserve leaders to handpick potential hires for them. An indicator of that effort's success took place during National Aboriginal Day on June 21, 2007, where Safeway sponsored at least a dozen events. Community leaders who attended expressed appreciation for Safeway and named people from their community who were also now part of Safeway's community.

People from their community are now part of Safeway's community: that story really resonates for me. It is important to appreciate that a workplace is, in fact, a community. When we consciously create workplaces that are "communities," we foster environments of connection and relationship. We share common values and norms of behaviour. In a workplace community that respects difference, that very respect becomes a community norm. It becomes part of who we are, and how we all behave. Individual differences do not separate or create barriers between us. We are part of the community of our workplace, the "us" that is the dominant group in our workplace.

As a result of relationships developed between the aboriginal and Safeway communities, a greater awareness and appreciation of aboriginal culture exists throughout Safeway. "Management is getting cognizant of the aboriginal culture," reports Yeo. "We had a manager who went to aboriginal awareness at the Justice Institute, then National Aboriginal Day. The employees called me to ask if they could dress down to fit in more with the community."

When we adjust our behaviour to "fit in" with the behaviour of others, we demonstrate respect to the members of that group. For years, members of our aboriginal communities were forbidden to practice their own traditions or openly manifest their differences. The message aboriginals habitually received was that they needed to fit in with non-aboriginals, the "dominant" group. When we are genuinely interested in demonstrating respect to those who are different than us, we need to go beyond tolerating their differences. We need to learn about and embrace those differences, and consistently demonstrate that we respect who they are by modifying our own behaviour. We need to ensure we are modelling respect.

Community involvement is a central focus of Safeway's diversity strategy. "We get involved in all the community celebrations. We look for the opportunities because we believe in supporting our communities," says Yeo. Safeway approaches them and typically supplies the food for the volunteer tents. Meanwhile, Safeway managers ask questions and engage in dialogue. They don't just ask "how are you?" They show a genuine interest in other cultures. "That," says Yeo, "is how we build relationships."

Safeway also actively recruits employees who are new immigrants to Canada. "About three years ago, we approached the Surrey/Delta Immigrant Society (now the Diversecity Community Resources

Society) to open up lines of communication," says Yeo. That evolved into Safeway giving presentations to other immigrant organizations in the Lower Mainland around Vancouver. "We tell them about Safeway: who we are, what kinds of jobs we have, what we offer, wages, benefits. It is a recruitment presentation. The interesting part is the Q and A after. The first question new immigrants always ask is whether they speak enough English [to get a job]. I say if we can have this conversation, the answer to that is yes."

Safeway has a sound business reason for reaching out into the community. When you are doing business or offering a service in a community, you want to attract members of that community to do business with you. Employees can encourage others from their community to do business with you. Beyond that, those employees can offer an employer a wealth of information on what products and services their community might want. That, too, helps the bottom line. Attracting and retaining diverse employees creates new business possibilities for employers.

SaskTel is another organization that welcomes opportunities to develop relationships with the communities it serves. It is a core business philosophy. "We all live in the same community, so we want to participate in those communities," says Carolynne Warner. "It is our customer base and our future employee base… We are also interested in being good neighbours." In some cases, community groups approach SaskTel for support. The company responds only in cases where those organizations will visibly foster diversity. Recent examples include the Federation of Saskatchewan Indian Nations and the North Central Family Centre in Regina. SaskTel also supports programs in local adult learning centres throughout the province of Saskatchewan.

"We have an aboriginal marketing segment, a team developed specifically to work with our customers in the aboriginal community and to be the bridge into the other parts of the organization," notes Warner. The company has partnered with a lot of organizations, having found that this assists in recruiting a diversity of employees. For instance, it has had a longstanding partnership with the Prince Albert Grand Council's virtual high school and other aboriginal organizations.

Another community-based organization is the SaskTel Pioneers, a group of employees who donate their time to different community programs. Employees are encouraged to get involved in many community events, from environmental and charitable causes to literacy awareness. "Nobody is required to participate, but they are encouraged to," says Warner, who adds that some of the hours are on work time.

The employee networks at SaskTel serve a dual function. "Each network has a business plan," explains Warner. "SAEN looks at how they can assist the company in providing service to the aboriginal customers, and then SEND does the same for persons with disabilities. The networks provide feedback either to the director of diversity... or to the manager of a particular department. They can suggest an event and the company can also alert them about an event. They also help with career fairs. We may request assistance or they may come forward."

Like at Safeway and KPMG, SaskTel's interest in diversity flows from a desire for superior business results. Says Warner, "It is all rolled up into the business case, and the focus is twofold. In order to be able to serve our customers better, we need to be able to reflect our customers. In order for our diverse employees to be able to participate to their full abilities, we have to have a workplace that embraces diversity or difference. We don't want everyone to contribute the same thing. We need a variety of contributions to come up with the best solution. We don't want everyone to think the same way. If everyone thinks the same way, it limits ideas and solutions."

Leaders at SaskTel appreciate that diversity is not an add-on strategy. They know it must become part of the corporate culture. As HR manager Carolynne Warner said, "Our intention is to have diversity woven into our culture, to have diversity be how we do things and define who we are. Diversity was incorporated into our competencies when they were written. It is not a separate department. It has become the way that we operate."

Employers of Choice understand that the respectful integration of difference into an organizational culture is an ongoing process. Changing a culture certainly is not an easy job. Consistency is so important.

When you are on the Road to Respect, when you adopt respect as a core value in your organization, you are by definition making a commitment to promote and embrace diversity. Leaders at SaskTel appreciated the importance of integrating respectful management of difference into their corporate culture and embarked upon a purposeful strategy to achieve that goal.

SaskTel started talking about diversity in 1990. The firm followed up initial conversations with company-wide diversity training co-facilitated by the company and the union. Later, SaskTel expanded training resources and made them available on request – including diversity training for both individuals and groups, and workshops about First Nations that focus on myths, misconceptions and company relationships with aboriginal communities. There have been courses on gender difference and a Respectful Workplace workshop. All these exist to promote SaskTel's corporate values: "respecting the differences in individuals and how to promote understanding."

One way SaskTel weaves diversity into its culture is by requiring both employees and teams to include a diversity objective in their development plans. All employees and leaders are held accountable for outlining and meeting their diversity goals, just as they are held accountable for meeting any other business objective. "The departmental plan states that each employee must have an individual plan," says Warner. "Every employee has a diversity objective in their annual review and it is included as part of performance management." Tailored to each individual, it may involve formal training if, for example, their customer base has changed. Or it may suggest they volunteer for a community event. Employees set diversity objectives as a team. They can request the Respectful Workplace workshop or another option, perhaps based on survey results or other feedback.

The organization frequently offers "lunch-and-learn" sessions for interested employees, with videoconferencing giving access to employees not at headquarters. "Several such sessions focused on First Nations and Métis heritage, culture and tradition, even the symbolism of the teepee. Invisible disabilities inspired an entire series. Others have talked about depression and bi-polar disorder. One even educated employees about wheelchairs for Rwanda, a community service partnership."

Besides the training courses, staff can access diversity training videos, particularly popular at departmental staff meetings.

For SaskTel, the key to culture change is constant reinforcement. The diversity message is reinforced in all the firm's videos, in the CEO's tours and in the firm's support for employees.

SaskTel's online weekly employee newsletter highlights SaskTel employees – sharing their stories, challenges and successes. It promotes a sense of connection and belonging as it celebrates differences large and small. Articles focus on employees' community work, family and workplace life, as well as health and safety issues.

A diversity strategy involves considerable effort and may cause short-term organizational upheaval. However, once these practices are established and consistently practiced, they're integrated into the corporate culture. "It is so woven into our culture now, it is hard to see how we do it," muses Warner of SaskTel. Respectful management of difference becomes self-sustaining, although it's key to ensure that these practices remain flexible and responsive. Our workplace communities will continue to change in the new millennium. Employees will join and depart, mergers may occur, new socio-political realities may rear their heads. However, once respectful practices are in place, the workplace culture will adjust and continue to prosper. A respectful culture is an adaptive culture.

KPMG embarked on its formal diversity initiative to achieve a competitive business advantage. Says Val Duffey, "We want to be viewed both internally and externally as an Employer of Choice. In our industry, competition for talent is fierce. We are interested in attracting the best and brightest. We want those individuals to experience a respectful and inclusive environment, a workplace where each will fit and succeed. We also want to be viewed by the business community as a business that is growing in that direction."

KPMG's core value of respect has guided it in structuring a diversity initiative. Dialogue has consistently been the dominant feature because KPMG is interested in involving everyone in the discussion. It is not about imposing a strategy, but about communicating the business case and then providing a safe environment for the discussion to take place. "We used the survey results as a platform to have conversations," explains Duffey. "What is going on? What is responsible for these differences? What are our values? What is diversity?"

Conversations started at the top, then slowly permeated throughout the organization. Rather than impose a fixed timeline, KPMG took the time needed to ensure that leaders would really buy in to the business case, which was about "enhancing the workplace experience for everyone."

KPMG had no interest in individuals following an imposed directive. The idea was to model respectful behaviour and allow enough time for dialogue until everyone had "bought in."

"Resistance is too strong a word for what we encountered," says Duffey. "We encountered assumptions." When those assumptions started to emerge, dialogue helped determine how to modify cultural practices to eliminate them.

KPMG's goal was to make diversity part of the culture's fabric. "We developed a robust communication strategy. We needed to let people know what we meant," says Duffey. That strategy included emails from the CEO, messages from organizational and local leaders, information on employee desktops, a diversity calendar, promotion of cultural inclusivity, and diversity celebrations. KPMG also placed a strong focus on conversations at the local level, in group meetings and focus groups.

KPMG promoted local conversations because, given it's a national organization, executives knew that different teams would have different diversity challenges. KPMG decided to develop resources and programs that each local could access as appropriate – a respectful approach to managing difference.

To further reflect their core value of respect, each local was given ownership and held accountable for developing local programs and initiatives. Human resources staff were asked to support each local by providing knowledge, resources and best practices.

First partners, then middle managers were asked to analyze their regions and "act as local champions for their office" while working with their leadership teams. Each office came up with an action plan, and the local leader was accountable. The focus was on local planning and networking, and on facilitated discussions. Local initiatives were designed to help people break down barriers. One office looked at their stats, then did some presentations, looked at their performance management process, talked about levelling the playing field and held consensus meetings.

Although KPMG already had a number of female partners, the diversity dialogue revealed that practices were still negatively impacting women throughout the organization. "Micro-inequalities – things that you don't even notice until you start talking about them," says Duffey. The firm realized that the female partners held less power than the male partners, and that too many women were leaving during their childbearing years. "We wanted to look at that and see what our priorities were."

Initially, KPMG aspired to level the playing field. Leaders created women's networks and business development for female employees. Over time, however, the diversity framework integrated the firm's mentoring program and other networks (including one that promoted career advancement) as well. "One initiative encourages partners to take a junior person along to business meetings. The result of these initiatives is that the entire employee population benefits," says Duffey.

We have all heard that famous business expression, "What gets measured gets managed." KPMG evaluates its progress on an ongoing basis. In addition to the firm's annual survey, leaders look at retention and promotion trends, engagement and connectivity.

Leaders are held accountable; there are consequences for not living the corporate values.

KPMG's next phase is a national diversity training program, for which the firm will contract external experts. Leaders are also in the process of designing a new series of lunch-and-learn workshops around how employees deal with prejudices and how the firm can level the playing field. "These lunch-and-learns will focus on how we behave together as colleagues," says Duffey. "What is appropriate? What about jokes? What about tolerating differences? We will look at the spectrum of behaviour. And we will focus on myth busting, on dispelling the myths."

KPMG appreciates that culture change is a slow process requiring ongoing commitment and consistency. Even though KPMG is already an Employer of Choice, Duffey emphasizes that the firm will continue its journey on the Road to Respect. "I don't want to be Pollyanna and say that we don't have work to do. We know we do. However, we also know we are trending in the right direction."

Leaders at Safeway also realize that the respectful management of difference is a journey rather than a destination. Despite having received the Catalyst and other awards, this Employer of Choice continues to expand its diversity initiative. "We have to keep evolving," says Cliff Yeo. There is a diversity board for each division and district. These "diversity councils" brainstorm new initiatives that keep the culture going.

Safeway's goal is to infuse diversity into its culture. To make sure that happens, executives constantly reinforce the importance of respect. Every conference call, meeting and internal broadcast mentions something about diversity. Store managers then incorporate that message into their meeting agendas. Safeway's intranet also offers a toolkit to guide managers on incorporating diversity discussions into staff meetings, and a diversity website.

Every store has a television in its lunchroom for the in-house broadcast, which can also download onto employees' computers. Each store gets asked every month for a success story, some of which involve what employees do outside of work. When one store holds a cultural event, it's featured for every store in the country to see.

Safeway looks for opportunities to become involved in community celebrations and holidays. Not only do the stores supply food for some events and highlight the occasions in their stores, but they've even developed a multicultural food calendar. At first, the calendar hung in managers' offices, but now they're in demand by customers and store employees alike.

Cliff Yeo was kind enough to give me one of Safeway's beautiful colour calendars. It celebrates both ethnic foods and the people who eat those foods. The front cover reads, "At Safeway, we recognize, celebrate and benefit from the uniqueness of each employee and customer. We value, respect and support these differences in our workplace. We strive to reflect this diversity in the communities we serve." Each month features at least one Safeway employee involved in an initiative related to diversity, as well as more general stories about inspiring employees. The calendars also include information on each holiday, descriptions of the traditional foods and their significances. The calendar is a creative and accessible way to share knowledge about difference while highlighting what celebrations and traditional foods have in common.

Besides participating in community celebrations, Safeway celebrates holidays in its stores, the holidays chosen varying by the ethnic makeup of the communities each store serves. For instance, in many Vancouver, British Columbia, stores, where there is a large Asian population, Chinese New Year features dragon dances in the stores. Customers can follow the dragon around the store, past Chinese New Year posters.

As awareness of difference becomes ingrained in the culture, changes in practice filter down to that "micro-inequality" level. Where Safeway used to supply employees with pizza when their store received special recognition for performance, now they offer a wider variety of foods.

Safeway has not yet included diversity training for all employees – only for workplace leaders. But those leaders are accountable for translating what they learn in the classroom into practices in the workplace. The leaders' training is co-facilitated by a line manager and a member of the human resources team because Safeway wants to signal that diversity is not a human resources initiative but a shared responsibility for all.

The main goal of the day-long, interactive leaders' training is to start a dialogue and raise awareness about respectful management of difference. "We recognize that everyone has prejudices. It is not about changing values and attitudes; it is about changing behaviours. We talk about where we want to get to. We don't tell them exactly how they get there." A video featuring Steve Burd, Safeway's CEO, figures into the training, along with a variety of activities and exercises. Trainers use real examples, tie everything back to the workplace and look at how different people learn, an aspect of diversity in itself. Leaders encourage discussion about invisible rules, men vs. women, sexual orientation and many other issues. Participants discuss cultural differences and how to incorporate those into Canadian culture, and watch a video about people with disabilities. The focus is about recognizing difference and not operating on assumptions. Employees are told, "Watch out for your biases. Pause, think and redirect."

Once employees have been trained, Safeway leaders have to demonstrate that they can manage differences in a respectful manner. Cliff Yeo tells an interesting story of how the training affected one manager and her employee: "A couple of years ago a woman was praying on the floor in the bathroom. The female manager came in and said 'what are you doing?' The employee replied, 'I need to pray.' The manager said, 'Okay, but not on the bathroom floor. Come into my office.'" That manager had been taught to ask questions, then work matters out with the employee.

Accountability, of course, is key to realizing a diversity strategy. Safeway keeps statistics to assist in tracking progress. Each member of the management team is evaluated by supervisors, employees and customers on his/her diversity practices. "How do you know if you are progressing if you don't measure?" asks Yeo. "If everybody feels like they are part of the team, there will be more job satisfaction and productivity... Multiculturalism has become part of the culture now. It is second nature to us."

Whenever I hear a variation of that that last statement, I feel inspired. Similarly, when Val Duffey advised me that complaints of discrimination and discriminatory harassment don't occur at KPMG "because they are at odds with the culture," it gave me a sense that human rights laws are realizing their potential.

Differences exist in our workplaces and those differences affect our business. Diversity management is about changing the way we have responded to difference, challenging assumptions we have about others who are different. It is about losing our fear and learning to understand, accept and respect difference so we can work together cohesively and productively.

Paradoxically, when we truly respect difference in our workplaces, a new kind of commonality emerges. We don't all look or act the same, but we share the same passion and commitment to our job, team and organization. We share similar approaches to conflict and problem solving. We are all willing to engage in dialogue with one another, regardless of place in the hierarchy. We show a consistency of respect and accountability for our behaviour.

Employees who feel respected, valued and supported are healthy, happy, engaged and productive. Such employees work for Employers of Choice. They'll also work for you when you start down the Road to Respect.

Part 3

The Roadmap to Respect

9

Charting the Course
for a Respectful Culture

The health of the eye seems to demand a horizon. We are never tired, so long as we can see far enough.

—RALPH WALDO EMERSON

S INCE YOU HAVE made it this far and are still reading, it is safe to assume that you chose door number one back in Chapter Two. You want to build a respectful workplace culture, a culture that can propel your organization to become an Employer of Choice on the Path to Profit. That is your goal, your vision. It is that vision, at this point out there somewhere on the horizon, that will keep you committed, energized and motivated when the going gets tough, which it inevitably will. Hopefully, the success stories I have shared in this book will keep you inspired and engaged on the journey to achieve your goal and realize your vision of a respectful and profitable organizational culture.

Pablo Picasso, one of the most innovative and original painters of our time, once said, "Good artists copy, great artists steal." While I don't want to get a reputation for promoting unlawful behaviour, please feel free to "steal" any of the respectful practices of Employers of Choice. That is precisely why I have included them in this book. I want you, the reader, to use, adapt and modify these respectful practices and behaviours in your organization. Employers of Choice shared their stories with me so that I could provide you with a "how to" guide to building a respectful and profitable workplace culture. This book is intended to become your "roadmap to respect," if you will.

The good news is that you have already taken the most important step, which is committing to the vision of a respectful workplace culture where employees love to work and employers make the profits they desire. The next step will be to determine how you are going to create that culture and achieve that vision. I wish I could provide you with a clear step-by-step "travel guide." The reality is that I can't. As we discussed in Chapter Five, we are not talking about creating "cookie cutter" cultures. Your journey on the Road to Respect must be designed based on the realities of your organization. Your particular point of departure as well as subsequent stops will vary depending on your organization and its current culture. It is not about finding the right path. It is about finding your path, one that will be right for your organization.

However, no matter what the business reality or state of a current culture, one mandatory stop at the outset must be adopting respect as a core organizational value. That value, along with others you adopt or re-commit to as you build your values-based culture, must serve as your organizational foundation as well as your compass on the Road to Respect. As we've learned from Employers of Choice, in a truly values-based culture, every business decision and practice must be aligned with corporate values.

Throughout this book I have stressed the importance of walking the talk of respect. However, before leaders start walking the Road to Respect, I suggest they do a lot of talking. The journey to a respectful workplace culture must begin with communication – with questioning, information gathering, information sharing and dialogue. Make sure that once you start talking, you also do a lot of listening. This will ensure that any and all communication reflects the newly adopted core value of respect.

Start the Dialogue to Build Respect

As we have learned from Employers of Choice, ongoing and inclusive dialogue is the foundation of a respectful workplace culture. Whatever a firm's current communication practices, or the state of their current culture, now is the opportune time to start thinking about and modelling respectful communication in the workplace. Look for opportunities to promote and foster respectful, curious and inclusive dialogue and discussion.

First, determine how to start the conversation; figure out who should be included and what questions need to be asked. Think about what is prompting the move in this direction at this point in the organization's history. Is the company responding to a problem or crisis? Is it growing or changing? Are you interesting in having a competitive business advantage? Convinced this is the "right" thing to do? Start the dialogue with those types of questions. Include whoever needs to be involved so that you get valid information. The answer to those questions should assist in determining your strategy moving forward.

Take sufficient time to consider a few other questions critical to success. Who are you as an organization? What characterizes you as a company? Do you have a corporate vision? Is it reflective of the company you want to become? Do you have corporate values? Are they relevant? Are your values expressed within your corporate culture?

We have seen how Employers of Choice live their core values, we've seen how their business philosophy flows from the requirement to translate those core values into everyday business practices. A respectful workplace culture is by definition a values-driven culture. To build a respectful workplace culture, your organizational values – values that all employees can embrace – must become the foundation of your organizational culture.

Finding values that all employees can embrace may be easier than you think. I recently participated in an exercise around ethical values, defined as words or ideas that help us choose the right thing to do. Respect is an ethical value. In this exercise each individual was given a paper that listed fourteen ethical values. The facilitator then divided us into a number of groups. First, each of us had to choose the five values that were most important to us. Then we had to tally our individual results and identify the five values that were most important to our group. Finally, all of the groups reported back and the facilitators identified the five values that the majority of the groups identified as most important.

The values that emerged were compassion, fairness, honesty, respect and responsibility. The facilitator then shared some information with us that quite frankly blew me away. Those five ethical values emerge consistently no matter who does that exercise. He produced graphs and charts that included the responses of very diverse groups of people.[1] Whatever our gender, age, ethnicity and nationality, it seems we share common ethical values.

This is one reason values-based cultures are so successful. It is our shared values that hold us together and guide our actions and behaviours. It was a powerful experience sitting in that room, looking around at all those different people, most of whom I had never met, and feeling a sense of commonality and connection. I can only imagine what it must have been like that day at Intuit when 500 employees starting talking about their organizational values.

Engaging in dialogue about corporate values is a great way to start on the road to building a respectful workplace culture. An exercise like that can get people talking and open the lines of communication across hierarchical lines. Remember that one of the most effective ways to create a safe and empowered workplace is to facilitate relationships throughout an organization.

However, as we discussed in Chapters Three and Six, if disrespectful behaviours are present in a workplace, fear will probably prevent employees from participating in dialogue. Because of the cultural disconnect we talked about in Chapters Two and Six, it may be that those contemplating this journey will not appreciate the extent to which fear can affect employees. If fear is a reality in your workplace culture, you need to understand this before you make any strategic decisions. You may choose to contain the visioning discussion to the upper echelons while you do some information gathering to assess the state of your current culture.

Figuring out where you are as a culture is a critical part of the first leg of your journey. As we discussed in Chapter Two, you have to know where you are before you can figure out how to get where you want to go. You might decide to conduct an employee survey, or convene focus groups. You may want to follow the example of Scott Cook at Intuit and close down your company for a day and get everyone involved. While Intuit used that process to develop corporate values, other organizations could use the process to gather information about corporate culture. Divide up participants, give everyone butcher block paper and have them capture the characteristics of the organizational culture as it exists. If you are not sure how to gather the information you need, get help, either in-house or external. Experts out there can assist and support you on this journey. Asking for help is a respectful practice to model as you build a respectful corporate culture.

Whatever process or strategy you decide on, start off by asking if what you are considering is respectful. Will this demonstrate respect to everyone involved? Once you start down the Road to Respect, everything you do must be aligned with that value. No matter what the state of your current culture, if you consistently model respect, you build credibility and trust. As credibility and trust build, fear diminishes.

Consider following the example of KPMG in initially containing the dialogue at the executive level to create a truly honest and respectful dialogue throughout the organization. If your vision is to be realized, everyone on the executive must be ready to model respectful behaviour. The commitment must start at the top. It is imperative to follow the example of Issy Sharp of Four Seasons, who ensured that every member of his senior team embraced his Golden Rule culture. "Enforcing our credo was the hardest part, and senior managers who couldn't or wouldn't live by it were weeded out. That was painful, but it had to be done,"[2] Sharp recalls.

When you are ready to initiate the dialogue with employees, start from a place of honesty and disclosure. The communication must be reflective of where you currently are. If you have decided to engage in information gathering, think about how to communicate that process. Avoid making too many grandiose and visionary statements about what you are doing and why you are doing it unless you are certain that the executive team is 100 percent committed to realizing the respectful corporate vision.

Remember, this is not about adopting "paper strategies." My experience is that the senior team's commitment can waver once they realize what they are committing to. As we established in Chapter Three, creating a respectful workplace culture requires a commitment to talk about and deal with difficult issues like prejudice, stereotyping, racism, sexism, equality, inclusion, language, communication, conflict, fear and power in the workplace. It requires stepping out of our comfort zones, and that is a step many are unwilling to take.

Once I was contracted to assist a large organization interested in building a respectful workplace culture due to survey results that showed an alarming increase in employee harassment. The employee relations group was not surprised by the survey results or my report after I'd spoken to employees about their workplace culture. They had heard it all before. They had even tried to communicate what they knew to upper echelon leaders. The problem was that senior managers seemed unwilling to hear what they had to say. Like at the company with the bullying manager we talked about in Chapter Six, the employee relations department hoped an external expert might achieve different results. In case you haven't figured it out, I was that external expert.

I learned that a command and control culture was very much

alive and well at this workplace. A whole lot of disrespectful behaviour was going on. Although there were lengthy and detailed policies about diversity and discrimination, employees from the "disadvantaged groups" routinely experienced harassment and discrimination. Bullies were protected and promoted. Employees who voiced concerns were labelled "problems." Issues were rarely resolved effectively and conflicts sometimes dragged on for years. Employees were fearful, discouraged, apathetic and disheartened. Despite all the company statements about promoting a respectful workplace, most employees with whom I spoke had no faith that anything would change. The entrenched hierarchical power structure had produced a wide cultural disconnect between those at the top and lower levels; fear and mistrust permeated at all levels.

Top brass issued a directive that the firm become a respectful workplace. The cultural subtext was that everyone had to look like they were on board. A lot of communication went out about the commitment to building a respectful workplace. Committees were formed, definitions worked on. On paper, it all sounded really good. Everyone wanted to toe the politically correct line. However, as so often happens, this organization had done a whole lot of talking without any real understanding of what would be involved in succeeding. Thus, it didn't matter who delivered the message about the reality of the workplace culture and what it would take to travel on the Road to Respect. Those in positions of power were not ready to hear it and start the journey.

If you are not sure what is going on in your workplace, or if you have not yet gotten the commitment of your senior team, think about how you can gather the information you need in a respectful manner. Think about how much information should be shared with employees. That involves communication – clear, direct and honest. Don't make promises or commitments you might not be able to honour.

Whatever methods you choose, ensure that your information gathering is comprehensive and thorough. As we have discussed, depending on the state of your current culture, employees may not be willing to tell you what you need to know right off the bat. A number of processes may need to take place over a period of months. Think about Safeway's leaders' philosophy "to do it right, not to be first on the block." Take the time to gather the information required to formulate a strategy that will build a truly respectful workplace culture.

Once you have gathered enough information to accurately assess the state of your current culture, decide your next steps while continually assessing communication strategies. I cannot over-emphasize the importance of paying close attention to corporate communication. As I mentioned in Chapter Seven, every situation I have dealt with in the past ten years was either caused or exacerbated by problematic, disrespectful or insufficient communication.

Err on the side of more frequent communication. If you are not sure where things stand, if you have not made any decisions about next steps, let the employees know that. You have an opportunity to model the core value of respect that you want to build into your culture every time you engage in organizational communication. Even if nothing else is happening, that one change in practice will have a huge effect on your culture. Keep employees in the loop. Wherever possible, look for opportunities to promote discussion and dialogue and build relationship, particularly across organizational and hierarchical lines.

If your information gathering reveals that you are ready to start talking about and defining your corporate values, the next step is determining how to structure that process. Since values are going to be the culture's foundation, these need to be in place before you start developing or evaluating workplace policies and practices. Whatever process you choose, it should model respect, which means it will be open, transparent and inclusive.

Developing corporate values may have to go on the back burner if information gathering reveals that disrespectful behaviour and the fear it creates is a serious problem. If this is the case, acknowledge what you have discovered and take visible, respectful action to deal with it.

Put Your House in Order: Deal with Disrespectful Behaviour and Adopt a Respectful Workplace Policy

At a bullying symposium I attended recently, I heard a participant express frustration with the fact that in his experience, highly or uniquely skilled individuals often get away with unacceptable and disrespectful behaviours. These individuals, he felt, routinely behave badly with impunity. He believed that these individuals' power gave them a sense of invincibility – to the point they could almost hold the organization they worked for hostage. On rare occasions when they were called on their bullying behaviour, they would – instead of acknowledging it – respond to the effect of, "Well, what are you going to do, fire me?" Assuming themselves indispensable, they put out that dare knowing full well that the organization will not respond.

My immediate reaction was, "Yes, they should be fired, absolutely." Just as all senior executives must demonstrate respect, taking action against those with disrespectful behaviour should not be negotiable. There can be no waffling on this point. At Employers of Choice, everyone is held accountable for this. "We have terminated employees for consistent disrespect of people," says Ellen du Bellay, vice president of learning and development at Four Seasons.

While I advocate dealing promptly and consistently with disrespectful behaviour, I do not advocate a disrespectful or power-based response. The key here is to take action that is visible and respectful. It is not about making statements about zero tolerance and firing people. Employers of Choice use feedback respectfully. If employees say there is a problem, the respectful response is to acknowledge that and let them know they have been heard. The first step involves honest communication. You have to come right out and tell employees what you have found out. You have to talk about the fact that there is disrespectful behaviour in the workplace and that this has become an organizational concern.

This is an opportunity to send a clear message about disrespectful behaviour and your workplace culture. Whether or not you have formulated all your values, if you are gathering information to chart your course on the Road to Respect, you should be committed to the core ethical value of respect. Now is the time to come right out and say that. Whether or not you have engaged in a vision building exercise, you can let employees know that your intent is to embrace respect as a core organizational value. Again, steer clear of lofty vision and values statements. Keep it simple. Be clear, focused and genuine. You must ensure that all employees understand that the organization is on the Road to Respect and there will be no deviation from that path.

Depending on what you have discovered, you may decide to do more information gathering, either with the whole organization, or with specific departments or teams. If so, let employees know that is the plan. Determine whether problems are systemic or isolated within certain areas. You might identify only one or two individuals as particularly problematic. Who they are and where they sit on the organization chart will assist you in figuring out the best approach to take.

At the same time, evaluate any organizational policies that may relate to disrespectful behaviour. Although having a policy has little influence on its own, Canadian law requires a policy addressing the legally disrespectful behaviours of discrimination and discriminatory harassment. A truly respectful workplace policy also covers workplace bullying as discussed in Chapter Six.

I want to be perfectly clear that I am not talking here about adopting policies for compliance reasons. As I've shared, Employers of Choice all have policies around disrespectful behaviour, but don't have to access them very often because these policies are supported by the culture. They formulate the commitment to a respectful culture, define and clearly outline behavioural expectations. This is why they exist. Of course, they mean nothing unless everyone is accountable for "living" the policies.

These policies flow from and support your core value of respect. If your information gathering reveals disrespectful behaviour, then workplace policies that speak directly to that behaviour are a must. In addition to dealing with isolated or particularly glaring problems, adopt, modify or refresh your policy to help with initiating dialogue about respectful behaviour. Define disrespectful behaviour so that everyone understands what it is and looks like. That dialogue should involve everyone throughout the organization. It can be structured in a variety of ways, including training sessions for leaders and/or employees.

To develop policies, you can rely on in-house expertise or hire an external expert. I am often hired to write policies for clients. I write Respectful Workplace policies that include sections on discrimination, discriminatory harassment, workplace violence, workplace bullying and interpersonal conflict. I write Respectful Workplace policies as opposed to anti-discrimination or harassment policies because I prefer to promote the proactive and visionary purpose of the policy.

Of course, one purpose of the policy is to provide a mechanism employees can use when they experience disrespectful behaviour. However, as I have been arguing throughout this book, the real value is in creating a respectful workplace culture so that employees won't have to access the policy because everyone behaves toward each other in a respectful manner. It is like an insurance policy; you have it in case you need it, but you hope you never do.

Your policy should be a vehicle to promote respect and empowerment. It should be the foundation for awareness, education, dialogue and skill building. Employees must recognize disrespectful behaviour and be empowered to hold themselves and others accountable for demonstrating it.

"Bullying behaviour might happen, but I think people would call their manager on it," says SaskTel's manager of human resources Carolynne Warner. "Some might say it directly, some might go to the union, but it would not be put up with. There is not a high tolerance level for inappropriate communications."

As discussed in Chapter Six, we are only just starting to understand what workplace bullying is and how covert and widespread it is. We need to promote awareness about this behaviour in our workplaces. Emerging research indicates that the majority of individuals who engage in bullying behaviour can change their behaviour with the help of workplace support. Change starts with dialogue about what is and is not respectful. Your policy can initiate that dialogue.

Leaders need to understand how to lead respectfully. They must be trained and supported to do so with practices like those we've discussed. A critical piece of dialogue on the Road to Respect focuses on power, and how to manifest and demonstrate power respectfully. Information gathering might reveal some power-based management in your organization. Again, rather than charge in with both barrels blazing, take the time needed to find out what is really going on and then make decisions based on what you learn about each individual situation. Take a coaching approach rather than a disciplinary approach. "We want to provide support. We want to save people. It costs a lot to retrain and recruit," says Jane Sillberg, director of human resources at Intuit Canada.

As we learned in Chapter Seven, Employers of Choice promote coaching throughout their organizations. Human resources professionals are trained to coach leaders, including members of the executive team. Managers are trained to coach their team members. Mentors coach their mentees. Coaching is by definition respectful. And it is an incredibly effective way to modify behaviour, much more effective than progressive discipline or counselling. Research on the impact of coaching shows that organizations reap average returns of 5–7 times the initial investment made in the coaching process. One study found that individuals with problematic behaviour who received coaching reflected a seventy-seven percent improvement in working relationships with direct reports, a seventy-one percent improvement in relationships with immediate supervisors, a sixty-seven percent improvement in teamwork, sixty-three percent improvement in working relationships with peers and sixty-one percent improvement in job satisfaction.[3]

Most workplace policies specify that employees with problem behaviours are subject to discipline "up to and including termination." That phrase comes from employment law. It is one I used a lot when I worked in labour relations and assisted managers in writing disciplinary letters. But when dealing with disrespectful behaviour, we should shift from an employment law paradigm to a human rights paradigm, and focus on remedying the problem as opposed to punishing the offender. We should start with supportive coaching and shift to a progressive disciplinary approach only when we determine that the employee we are coaching is not interested in or capable of modifying his or her behaviour. When it's clear that an employee will not conform to the expected norms of the respectful workplace culture, that is the time to take action, in some cases disciplinary action, to end the employment relationship.

While interpersonal conflict is not a form of disrespectful behaviour, I always include a section on it in my Respectful Workplace policies. Think and talk about conflict management as you make your way on the Road to Respect. Conflict is a naturally occurring phenomenon bound to occur at work, possibly even more so these days in light of workplace diversity. Conflict must not be avoided or feared. It should be recognized for what it is: a sign that something is wrong and that action, generally discussion, needs to take place. A safe working environment promotes constructive conflict, which encourages and welcomes the expression of divergent opinions. Everyone should be able to contribute to the productivity and profitability of your business.

A lot of pieces need to be in place to support an effective conflict management system – the absence of fear and a foundation of trust being two of the most critical. However, even if conditions are not yet ideal in your workplace, a policy focused on interpersonal conflict sets up expectations around respectful resolution of conflict. It allows you to talk about conflict and how it manifests within organizations. I cannot tell you the number of times I hear employees tell me about "irresolvable" conflicts at work. For many, the idea of approaching another individual to discuss a concern is inconceivable. Fear of "confrontation" often prompts unwillingness to take action. For many of us, talking to someone with whom we have a conflict automatically becomes a confrontation. I think this is because most employees do not have the communication skills to respectfully frame issues in a conflict. As we have learned, in a respectful workplace culture, employees are held accountable for resolving conflicts and raising issues of concern to them. A good conflict management policy provides the framework from which to promote this behaviour and associated skill development among employees.

It is also the foundation of my Respectful Workplace policies. Most discrimination and harassment policies I have read require or suggest that employees try to resolve their issue by first directly approaching the other person and telling them they want the behaviour to stop. However, if the culture does not support employees approaching each other when they have simple conflicts, what are the chances they will do so when faced with seriously disrespectful and often power-based behaviours like discrimination, harassment or bullying?

Respectful resolution of conflict at work is a cultural issue. Employees will approach each other to discuss problems only when that becomes the cultural norm. Adopting a policy allows us to create the expectation of the behaviour. We then develop that behaviour through corporate practices, including coaching, training and modelling respectful conflict resolution.

I also encourage clients to consider including Respectful Workplace guidelines in their Respectful Workplace policy. These are in effect a code of conduct. Many of us instantly recoil at the idea of a code of conduct. We are unfortunately living in an era of overregulation which can promote fear, bureaucracy and organizational paralysis. I am not interested in promoting more rules and regulations within organizations. I am advocating respectful, adaptive, responsive and flexible cultures, not ones weighted down in policies and procedures.

That said, in the reality of our diverse multicultural workplaces, Respectful Workplace guidelines provide an opportunity to elaborate on what respectful behaviour looks like. Rather than a series of rigid rules, these guidelines can and should serve as a foundation for dialogue and discussion. We cannot allow the plethora of behaviours that are now acceptable in society to become part of our corporate culture if we are interested in having a respectful workplace.

A couple of years ago I wrote a newsletter called "Let's Talk About Sex" after walking into the corporate office of a client and finding myself confronted by the gaping cleavage of a receptionist. In that newsletter I advocated a corporate dress code and dialogue about respectful and professional dress at work. My policies generally include these guidelines, particularly for corporate clients. How can you make statements about a workplace free of sexual harassment while allowing employees to dress in a manner that invites ogling and staring? If we are serious about building a respectful workplace culture, we have to talk about this stuff. Developing and adopting a guideline provides the ideal opportunity to start the conversation.

Leaders can frame discussions in focus groups, lunch-and-learns, team meetings and formal training. Choose what works for your organizational reality. You might adopt a policy and then provide formal training if you believe fear might prevent more informal dialogue at this point in the process. You might include employees in the process of developing your policy and guidelines. At the end of the day, however, if you are going to realize your vision of a respectful workplace culture, you will need organizational policies that support the development of that behaviour as a norm within your workplace.

Align Your Business with Your Values

As we have learned from Employers of Choice, culture change takes considerable time; it's an ongoing business reality, not a one-time process. Because change can be scary stuff, it is important to develop a strategy to manage change respectfully. That goes back to the importance of ongoing discussion and dialogue, and looking for opportunities to promote respectful communication and build trust and relationship.

While organizations need to look at every business practice

and policy, this book focuses on people practices, which most organizations regard as human resources or employee relations department responsibilities. But human resources employees are often isolated within their department until notified that there's a problem with which they need to deal. Jane Sillberg of Intuit noted that often, the role of human resources is to ensure the organization is complying with laws and regulations. Its focus is reactive as opposed to proactive.

Employees who work in human resources at Employers of Choice do much more than just react when there is a problem. They do more than merely make sure the law is being followed. They work proactively to promote and support the business and its respectful culture. They have a key strategic business function. Unfortunately, other firms' human resources departments are not integrated into the business, and human resources staff are rarely empowered as change agents. In many cases, staff in human resources possess a lot of information about the business and employees that leaders never hear or access.

One stop on your journey should involve examining your organizational structure to determine whether it will support the respectful culture you now envisage. Too many organizations are based on hierarchical, command and control and/or linear models that may have outgrown their usefulness. Evaluate your organizational structure's flexibility and responsiveness, and how it influences information and communication. You want an organizational structure that promotes relationship building across hierarchical lines, and encourages responsibility and accountability. You want to promote dialogue and information sharing within and between departments and teams. The larger your company, the more complex that may be, but it is critical to find a way to promote that type of connection and responsiveness regardless of your size.

The role of your human resources department must be to promote and support people practices that build a respectful culture. It should be structured and aligned to actively promote the success of the business. In almost every business, employees are the greatest asset. If you want to remain on the Path to Profit, it is imperative that your organizational structure ensures that employees are focused, engaged and committed to your business goals while human resources staff act as organizational guides and coaches by promoting the people practices that support building a respectful and profitable workplace culture.

In Chapter Five we talked about respectful hiring practices and aligning hiring practices with the business culture. Hire for your desired culture throughout your organization, including within human resources, perhaps after gathering information focused on the human resources role within your organization. What is it that these employees are doing and what else could they be doing? What is their function within the organization and does it need to shift or change? What are the qualities you need in the individuals working to support your desired culture?

At Intuit, they know exactly who they want working in their HR department. "For the last HR business partner, the recruiter screened eighty-two people before she presented anyone," says Jane Sillberg. "We have a value: Seek the best. They know how critical it is to have the right person in the right job. HR are compensated at a manager's level or above. They have high skills. We look for a business background as well as HR skills. They are coaches as well as managers."

Whether or not you decide to adopt Intuit's business model of placing human resources employees within the business unit, think about how to promote relationship between those who work in HR and the employees they are hired to support. Four Seasons structures human resources as the hotel's social centre. That's to build relationship and foster connection and community. The key is determining the human resources business model that will work for your organization, to support you in achieving your organizational vision.

Information gathering should give you a clear picture of the "life cycle" of your employees. What is the employee experience, starting with their first employment interview? How is the orientation program structured? How are employees integrated into their work teams and job functions? Are they mentored and if so, how are those relationships structured? Do they attend formal training? What does that training look like? How is their performance measured? What is their experience of internal promotion and advancement? Are employees reporting to managers or leaders? What types of relationships are developed among employees, within their teams, with their supervisors or subordinates, with individuals in other departments? What types of opportunities are created to get and give feedback within the team? Are employees engaged and interested in what they are doing while at work? Do organizational practices support them or hinder their productivity? Is there a sense of connection to the workplace? Are employees having fun; do they enjoy being in the workplace?

Although you will be evaluating many different organizational practices along your journey, the process you use to align your practices to your values will be structurally similar. In every case, you must start with discussion, dialogue and information gathering, and include examination, assessment and realignment.

At some point in your journey, you will be ready to ask the questions we looked at in Chapter Eight around managing difference in your workplace. This dialogue may start when you adopt your Respectful Workplace policy, or when you start talking about respectful leadership practices. It might result from what you discover in your information gathering. You may learn of "micro-inequalities" within your corporate culture as KPMG did, and start the dialogue from there. You might develop new polices and practices around diversity management as Safeway did when it adopted the Championing Change for Women initiative. You might want to look at how you can develop relationships with the community to assist you in attracting the diverse population you are seeking.

Over time, curiosity, questioning and ongoing evaluation will start to become a norm within your organization. While initially everyone will be supported and coached to embrace the organizational changes, those who cannot or will not adapt to your vision of a respectful workplace will be eliminated. Employees will begin to lose their fear as disrespectful behaviours slowly diminish and respectful practices continually grow. The ongoing communication and dialogue will promote the development of relationship, trust and connection between employees. The integration of practices that support the respectful management of difference will empower employees to express themselves and fully contribute to their work and teams. Employees will be held accountable for raising issues and concerns, and will be supported in doing so. Slowly, the "way it is around here" will change as respectful practices become woven into the fabric of your organizational culture.

A respectful workplace culture is by definition a dynamic, learning culture. The learning is a byproduct of the ongoing questioning and dialogue that becomes part of your organizational culture and business model. That same dialogue ensures that your organization remains adaptable and responsive to external changes that affect your business. It ensures that you become an Employer of Choice with a respectful culture that attracts and retains talented, engaged and committed employees. The Road to Respect is the Path to Profit.

Respect and the Unionized Workplace

Two Employers of Choice with whom I spoke, SaskTel and Safeway, are unionized, and some Four Seasons hotels are unionized. When I interviewed these organizations I asked them to describe their relationships with their union and reveal how the union figured into the development of their culture.

Having spent years doing labour work both at the airline and in my consulting practice, I have worked within and observed the gamut of union management relationships. Some are more respectful and/or collaborative than others. This book has spent a lot of time looking at the relationship between power and disrespectful behaviour within organizations. The reality is that most unions are structured in a linear, hierarchical fashion. Unions have also evolved from, or may have consciously adopted, a traditional command

and control model. The same types of disrespectful, power-based behaviours and relationships found in workplaces are present in many unions. Within a unionized workplace, a union official has a position of power and can choose to manifest that power respectfully or disrespectfully.

I certainly learned a lot about union management relationships when I worked for the airline. Admittedly, I started off with a bit of an idealistic attitude about how those relationships should work. I came from an academic background where we savoured a steady diet of collaborative relationships and win/win negotiations, worshiping at the feet of Roger Fisher and William Ury, whose bestselling book, *Getting to Yes*, was the holy book of labour relations in the 1980s.

After working at the airline for a while, I concluded that union management relationships were really all about manifesting power within a specific structural paradigm – the us-and-them, adversarial, win/lose paradigm. It was rarely about working together to create a bigger pie. It was always about the size of each party's slice. We often needed concessions from our unions to bring costs down and in those situations it was very clear who had the power and who didn't, who was the winner and who was the loser.

As much as we tried to talk about building collaborative relationships, the evidence of us-and-them was everywhere. I constantly had managers referring to the collective agreement as "the union book." Much as I tried to emphasize the fact that the collective agreement was in fact negotiated between the parties, managers saw the provisions as "union" rules getting in the way of running things the way they wanted.

Within the labour department, we worked to form collaborative relationships with our unions. There were definitely some success stories. However, both the company and unions were very large and weighed down by history, bureaucracy and entrenched patterns of behaviour. That made it very challenging to shift from a win/lose adversarial paradigm to the Ury and Fisher collaborative win/win paradigm. Looking back on it now, I see that the union/

management relationship was very much a reflection of the cultures of both the airline and its unions.

One thing I could clearly see at the time, however, was that the dynamic of union management relationships at the airline was very much influenced by the overall lack of communication between the union and anyone who did not work within the labour department. The human resources department was completely separate from the labour department. The organizational structure was such that the labour department was "responsible" for dealing with the unions. Each labour advisor had internal clients whom we would counsel about collective agreement interpretation. Rather than talk to their local stewards, most management personnel would call us to ask us what a certain clause or specific word or phrase meant. They would also call us when their local union representative would get all hot and bothered about something they did that violated the collective agreement – which in many cases they had not bothered to consult because it was "the union book."

Within our department we often talked about how more training within the management group would nurture relationships and trust between management and the union. We were constantly cleaning up messes that resulted from someone in the company doing something without first involving the union. A decision would be made, a decision that affected unionized employees, but most of the time no one outside the labour department would think about talking to the union ahead of time. Or if they did think about it, fear and mistrust made them hesitate to actually do it. When there was communication, it arose during planned meetings with individuals from both sides. The concept of respectful communication was nowhere on the radar. Unfortunately, we were always too busy cleaning up the messes to focus on how to prevent the messes in the first place.

Actually, one of those messes prompted management to offer me the human rights portfolio. When I left for maternity leave, a human resources employee in charge of administering human rights policy decided to leave the airline and start a consulting practice.

She concluded that her transition to self employment would be a lot smoother if she could retain the business of the airline as her major client. Her boss supported her plan.

The airline's human rights policy had been jointly negotiated between the unions and the company. Needless to say, when the unions caught wind of the fact that they were now supposed to deal with a private contractor as opposed to an airline employee – and that they had not been consulted about this change – the proverbial you-know-what hit the fan. One of the vice chairs of the IAM, the machinists union, stormed into my boss's office, dumped more than sixty harassment files on her desk and announced that the IAM would no longer deal with human resources on these files. They were going to revert to the previous practice of dealing with the labour department. Not one to waste time, my boss called me later that day and offered me the departing staffer's position. While it worked out well for me, I imagine it threw a bit of a wrench into that former employee's business plan.

I share this story as an example of what so often goes wrong, not only in union management relationships, but in all relationships. It is a failure to communicate, a failure to engage in meaningful dialogue. It is not possible to establish a collaborative, trusting relationship without ongoing and respectful dialogue. In a respectful workplace culture, the management/union relationship can be no different than any other business practice. It must be aligned with values, must be respectful.

Unionized employers on the Road to Respect should approach their union management relationship in the exact same manner as they do every other business practice. Start with questioning, information gathering and dialogue. Involve whoever needs to be included in the discussion. Analyze practices and relationship. Figure out where the organization is and then map out a strategy to get to where you want to be.

Recently an employer from a unionized workplace who attended one of my workshops used information from it to initiate a dialogue with the union. He wanted to create a respectful workplace and adopt a corporate policy that protected employees from being bullied at work. The union representative completely supported his interest and the parties agreed to incorporate language on workplace bullying into the collective agreement.

I have been involved in situations where unions supported employers who took a strong stand against bullying, even when the bullying involved two union members. Most unions are interested in working with an employer to eliminate disrespectful, power-based behaviours. I believe that client's experience is typical of what one can expect when employers invite their union to join them in promoting a more respectful workplace.

It happens at unionized Employers of Choice. "We have a very good working relationship with all three of our unions at Safeway," says human resources advisor Cliff Yeo. "It is a collaborative relationship." Whether communicating through joint committees or in more formal ways, he feels there is "a mutual interest in promoting a diverse workplace. Our union has the same mindset with respect to diversity. They have female management, and they are also multicultural."

Carolynne Warner, manager of human resources, says SaskTel respects the role that its union plays. "We give the union a heads-up about things that are happening... The union comes as a guest speaker to the manager's industrial relations training [and] we have a number of joint committees." She says SaskTel encourages employees to use the union as a resource.

A respectful union management relationship does not mean a relationship without disagreement or conflict. But as long as there is dialogue and an interest in resolving an issue, the process and relationship reflect respect.

A union's *raison d'etre* is to protect workers and improve working conditions. Unions and the employees they represent stand to benefit when an employer chooses to travel on the Road to Respect. To travel that road, make the union your partner. The relationship will be paved with respect and the result will be a true win/win for the business, union and employees.

10

Leading the Change

Example is not the main thing in influencing others. It is the only thing.

—ALBERT SCHWEITZER

WIKIPEDIA DEFINES LEADERSHIP as an individual's ability to influence, motivate and enable others to make their organizations more effective and successful. Visionary and committed leadership is the most critical factor shared by Employers of Choice. Such leadership has allowed those companies to achieve both their desired respectful corporate culture and their business success in general.

Creating an organizational culture, and in particular changing a corporate culture, cannot occur without visionary and committed leaders. In some organizations, one leader like Issy Sharp or Scott Cook can make the difference. In other organizations, a small group of committed leaders like at KPMG may initiate the process. Either way, these leaders inspire and motivate scores of others to embrace the change required to build a truly respectful workplace culture. They also create truly adaptive and cohesive, values-based cultures that ensure ongoing profitability.

Not an easy thing to do. Holding onto a good culture requires being both inflexible on core adaptive values and flexible regarding most practices and other values, note Kotter and Heskett of Harvard Business School. "It requires pushing hard to win, but not allowing the pride that comes with success to develop into arrogance. And it requires providing strong leadership, yet not strangling or smothering delicate leadership initiatives from below."[1]

Building a respectful culture demands committed leadership. A culture change initiative will simply not succeed without the right leadership. How is your culture change going to happen? Who is going to be at the helm of this journey of culture building?

Maybe it will be you. If you are a workplace leader – in particular a senior leader or member of the executive team – I believe this book will serve you well. Creating a respectful workplace culture is simply a business necessity in today's diverse and multicultural workplace. I hope that the stories of successful Employers of Choice I've shared have proven inspiring. I hope they've made you want to follow their example and become a leader who chooses to model respect. Hopefully you're eager to put on your walking shoes and start down the Road to Respect. I congratulate you on your choice and wish you the best on your journey. If I can be of any assistance along the way, please don't hesitate to call.

If, on the other hand, you are not senior management, you certainly have not wasted your money on this book. Scores of individuals without traditional leadership titles learn to demonstrate leadership and wield power. Executives may be powerful, but as we have discussed, it is how they use that power that determines whether or not they are a true, respectful leader.

According to Warren Bennis, pioneer in the field of leadership studies, "Leaders are people who do the right things." Given that you picked up this book, I have to conclude you wish to do the right things.

In Chapter Eight I talked about kicking off training sessions by asking participants whether or not they think a person can train someone to be respectful. I use that opening question to initiate a dialogue about power and choice. I like to get that out in the open right away – to let participants know that what we are really talking about is power and how we choose to use our power. We can use our power to promote respectful behaviour or disrespectful behaviour. We can pretend we don't have any power; we can choose to feel victimized by disrespectful behaviour. Or we can choose to watch passively as others are victimized by it.

On the other hand, we can decide to recognize that no matter where we sit on the organizational chart, we have power, and we can use that power to promote respectful behaviour in our workplace.

You might be someone who can initiate the necessary dialogue that will inspire leaders to embark down the Road to Respect. Now that you have read this book, you have the knowledge, an important source of personal power. You can make a very compelling argument for why adopting respect as a core value in a values-based culture is the Path to Profit in today's multicultural, diverse and global marketplace.

Maybe you work in human resources. Maybe you are a manager, team leader or union representative. Even if you can't change the entire workplace culture, you can start off by focusing on the subculture in your particular area. You can look around for evidence of disrespectful behaviour within your work group and observe your own behaviour when you are involved in or observing a conflict. You can become curious about whether or not micro-inequalities exist in your organization.

If you are directing others, you can start to think about your own leadership style. You can initiate a dialogue with subordinates about respectful behaviour. You can ask for feedback about your leadership style. You can engage in a similar type of dialogue with your peers and colleagues, and even those to whom you report.

What if you are someone without any positional power at all?

Please, don't throw up your hands and say, 'Well, what can I do?' There is a lot you can do. I recently read a story about a woman who had been working for a bullying supervisor for years.[2] As typically happens, everyone in the department spent a good deal of their time complaining about this supervisor. One day this woman was talking to a friend about her situation and her friend suggested that she try initiating a conversation with the problematic individual. She decided she had nothing to lose and the next day asked her supervisor how things were going. To her surprise, her supervisor was amenable to engaging in a friendly conversation. She continued to look for opportunities to talk with her supervisor, and slowly, a relationship developed. She learned that her supervisor had been feeling incredibly pressured and isolated and was really grateful for the opportunity to talk. Like a pebble thrown into a pond creating a ripple that gets wider and wider, this one action had an ongoing effect in her workplace. The supervisor became visibly more relaxed. Everyone in the department noticed the change in her demeanour and benefited from it. As a result of that one woman's choice, they all experienced a more respectful workplace.

In *The Power of Tact*, businessman Peter Legge asks, "What if we started taking tiny steps to treat each other with more respect... What effect do you think that would have on the world that we live in?"[3] That is a no-brainer for me. I know the effect it would have. It would create a more respectful world, one which we would all be more comfortable and happier living in. And now that you have read this book, you know that too.

To create a truly respectful workplace culture, everyone in the organization must embrace the core cultural value of respect. A respectful workplace is a culture of leadership. Each individual must choose to adopt respect as a core personal value, and model that in everything he or she does. It means making a commitment to be respectful both to yourself and others. It means embracing that value not only when you are at work, but in your life.

The journey on the Road to Respect is both an organizational and a personal journey. No matter who you are, you can make a choice to take that journey, to lead by example, to model respectful behaviour and inspire others to do the same. Be the leader of your life. Choose to walk the talk of respect.

Notes

Chapter 1

1,2 Issy Sharp, Rotman School, April 11, 2002. Rotman Integrated Thinking Seminar Series.

3 "Best Companies Offer Diversity-Related Lessons," Rebecca R. Hastings, *SHRM Online*, January 2007.

4,5 Four Seasons website.

Chapter 2

1 An initiative of the Vancouver Board of Trade, the Leaders of Tomorrow (LOT) is a pioneering student mentor program that connects post-secondary students from all disciplines with members of Vancouver's business community. Each year, LOT accepts only 100 students to participate in this program. www.boardoftrade.com

2 *Corporate Culture and Performance*, John P. Kotter, James L. Heskett, The Free Press, Simon &Schuster Inc., 1992.

3 *The Bully at Work*, Gary Namie and Ruth Namie, 2000, 2003.

4 *Native Son*, Richard Wright, 1940.

5 "The (Not So) Hidden Costs of Illness: Building Better Business Through Wellness," Anne Dranitsaris, PHD, *PeopleTalk Magazine*, Vol. 11, No. 3, Fall 2008.

Chapter 5

1 *Love 'Em or Lose 'Em, Getting Good People to Stay*, Beverly Kaye, Sharon Jordan-Evans, Berrett-Koehler Publishers, 2005.

Chapter 6

1 WorkDoctor.com

2 Laing arbitration – re: Government of Province of BC and BCGEU (M, G & Z Respondents), 1996, 49 L.A.C. (4th) 193 (Heather Laing).

3 "Bullies in the Workplace: A Focus on the 'Abusive Disrespect' of Employees," Teresa A. Daniel, *SHRM Online*, August 2006.

4   "£800,000 Payout for Bullied City Secretary," Adam Fresco, *London Times*, Tuesday, August 1, 2006.

5   "Bullying at Work Affects Seven in 10 People," Greg Pitcher, *Personnel Today.com*, March 7, 2008.

6   "Bad Boss, Bad Boss," December 2006 and "Mob Mentality," June 2007, *BCBusiness* magazine.

7   "Bullies in the Workplace: A Focus on the 'Abusive Disrespect' of Employees," Teresa A. Daniel, SHRM *Online*, August 2006.

8   "Bad Boss, Bad Boss," *BCBusiness* magazine, December 2006.

9   "Bullies in the Workplace: A Focus on the 'Abusive Disrespect' of Employees," Teresa A. Daniel, SHRM *Online*, August 2006.

10 "New workplace regulations target bullies," the *Vancouver Sun*, Wednesday, June 18, 2008.

11 *Shaw v. Xerox Canada Ltd.*, March 20, 2000, Ontario Court of Appeal.

12 *Keays v. Honda Canada Inc.*, March 17, 2005, Ontario Superior Court of Justice. (This case was appealed to the Supreme Court of Canada. On June 27, 2008 in a split 7:2 decision, the court overturned the decision of the Ontario Court of Appeal, further reducing the damage award.)

13 *Sulz v. Attorney General of Canada and Government of British Columbia*, January 19, 2006, BC Supreme Court.

14 Madam Justice Freda M. Steel, Manitoba Court of Appeal, Presentation for the Canadian Association for the Prevention of Discrimination and Harassment in Higher Education (CAPDHHE) conference, Winnipeg, Manitoba, 2002.

Chapter 7

1   *Corporate Culture and Performance*, John P. Kotter and James L. Heskett, The Free Press, Simon & Schuster Inc., 1992.

2   "The Feedback Sandwich is Out to Lunch, Time to Embrace the Main Course," Shelle Rose Charvet, *Speaking of Impact*, Winter 2007.

Chapter 8

1,2 "Cultivating Female Leaders," Ann Pomeroy, HR *Magazine*, SHRM *Online*, February 2007.

3   Steve Burd, Acceptance Speech, Catalyst Award, May 16, 2006.

4   "Diversity Training Motives Questioned by Report," Rebecca R. Hastings, SPHR, July 2007.

5   *If All Else Fails, Laugh!*, Suzie Humphreys, Tivydale Press, 2005.

6   *When You're About to Go off the Deep End Don't Take Your Kids with You*, Kelly E. Nault, Stepping Stones for Life Ltd., 2004.

7   *The Authoritarian Roots of Corporate Diversity Training*, Dr. Carl F. Horowitz, National Legal and Policy Centre, July 2007.

8   "2006 Catalyst Census of Women Corporate Officers and Top Earners of the FP500 in Canada," Catalyst Research Reports, Catalyst.org, April 2007.

9   "The Bottom Line: Corporate Performance and Women's Representation on Boards," Lois Joy, PHD, director, research, and Nancy M. Carter, PHD, vice president, research, at Catalyst Inc.; Harvey M. Wagner, PHD, and Sriram Narayanan, PHD, Catalyst Research Reports, Catalyst.org, October 2007.

10, 11, 12   "Cultivating Female Leaders," Ann Pomeroy, HR *Magazine*, SHRM *Online*, February 2007.

13   "Hotel and Disabled Workers Initiative," Richmond, Honorable Claude, Minister of Employment and Income Assistance, Vancouver, BC, April 2007.

Chapter 9

1   The Institute for Global Ethics (Canada), Colin McDougall, training consultant.

2   Issy Sharp, Rotman School, April 11, 2002. Rotman Integrated Thinking Seminar Series.

3   "Pruning Thorns from Roses," SHRM White Paper, Peter Adebi, MSA, SPHR, February 2008, SHRM *Online*, May 2008.

Chapter 10

1   *Corporate Culture and Performance*, John P. Kotter and James L. Heskett, 1992.

2   "Difficult Bosses: Taming the Dragon Lady with Courage and Compassion," Gary Harper, Gary Harper and Associates, 2007.

3   *The Power of Tact*, Peter Legge, Eaglet Publishing, 2008.

Employers of Choice

Four Seasons Hotels and Resorts

Intuit

KPMG

SaskTel

Canada Safeway

Four Seasons Hotels and Resorts

Founded in 1960, Four Seasons has followed a targeted course of expansion, opening hotels in major city centres and desirable resort destinations around the world. Currently with eighty-two hotels in thirty-four countries, and another thirty+ properties under development, Four Seasons continues to lead the hospitality industry with innovative enhancements, making business travel easier and leisure travel more rewarding.

Awards & Recognition

Fortune magazine (2008)
For the eleventh consecutive year Four Seasons was included in *Fortune* magazine's list of the "100 Best Companies to Work For." It is also considered an "All Star" company by the magazine, as it is one of only fourteen organizations that have been on the list every year since it launched in 1998.

Zagat Survey – World's Top Hotels, Resorts & Spas 2007/08
Four Seasons Hotels and Resorts was once again the top choice for travellers to the United States. In the 2008 Zagat Survey of Top U.S. Hotels, Resorts and Spas, Four Seasons was named number one hotel chain.

Travel + Leisure – World's Best (Aug. 2008)
In *Travel + Leisure*'s 2008 World's Best Awards Readers' Poll, Four Seasons hotels captured eighteen slots among the "Top 100 Hotels".

Condé Nast Traveler Reader's Choice Awards (Nov. 2008)
In 2008, fourteen Four Seasons properties ranked in the Top 100 List.

American Automobile Association
Twenty-three Four Seasons hotels and resorts won the AAA Five Diamond Awards for 2009 and five Four Seasons restaurants received Five Diamond Awards.

Gallivanter's Guide (Jan. 2008)
In the 2008 Gallivanter's Awards for Excellence, Four Seasons Hotels and Resorts have multiple awards including Number One spots as:
>Best Hotel Group Worldwide – Four Seasons Hotels and Resorts
>Best City Hotel Worldwide – Four Seasons Hotel George V, Paris
>Best European City Hotel – Four Seasons Hotel George V, Paris
>Best European Resort – Four Seasons Resort Provence at Terre Blanche
>Best Hotel/Resort in the Middle East/Africa – Four Seasons Resort Sharm El Sheikh
>Best City Hotel in North America – Four Seasons Hotel New York
>Best Spa Worldwide – Four Seasons Resort Provence at Terre Blanche
>Best Hotel/Resort Cuisine Worldwide – Four Seasons Hotel George V, Paris

Institutional Investor, World's Best Hotels (Nov. 2008)
Seventeen properties were listed in *Institutional Investor*'s "The Top 100 Hotels of the World."

Information about Four Seasons included in Road to Respect was gathered from interviews Erica conducted with Ellen du Bellay, vice president, learning and development, Four Seasons Hotels and Resorts, as well as from written materials provided to Erica by Ms. du Bellay. Any other sources used are identified with a footnote.

Intuit

Intuit Canada is headquartered in Edmonton and has employees in Calgary, Toronto, Ottawa and Montreal. Intuit Canada Limited is a premier innovative growth company that empowers individuals and businesses, and those who serve them, to achieve their dreams. Intuit Canada drives continuous growth by creating or acquiring easy to use connected services that create delight by solving important unsolved customer problems and build durable advantage. Key products and services include Quicken®, QuickBooks®, QuickBooks® Succès PME, QuickTax, and ImpôtRapideMC.

Awards & Recognition

Fortune magazine
Called Intuit "America's Most Admired Software Company" and one of the "100 Best Companies to Work For."

50 Best Employers in Canada
The *Globe and Mail's Report on Business* publishes the list of the Best Employers in Canada, with Intuit ranking #11 in 2007 and #9 in 2008.

Best Workplaces in Canada (Top 50)
The Great Place to Work® Institute Canada, in partnership with the *Globe and Mail*, publishes an annual Best Workplaces in Canada List, ranking Intuit #18 in 2006 and #16 in 2007.

Canada's Top 100 Employers
Mediacorp Canada Inc. announces list in special issue of *Maclean's* magazine, with Intuit ranked one of the Top Employers for 2002, 2003, 2004, 2005, and 2007. Intuit also received Alberta's Top 35 ranking in 2007.

Alberta's Top 35 and Canada's Best Diversity Rankings (2008)
Twenty-five of Canada's most widely recognized and successful companies recognized by BMO Financial Group and TWI Inc. for leading the nation in creating diverse and inclusive workplaces and to encourage other companies across Canada to adopt similar best practices.

ASTech Awards (2007)
The Alberta Science and Technology Leadership Foundation recognized Intuit for Outstanding Commercial Achievement in Alberta Science and Technology – Businesses with gross sales over $25M (FY06).

Alberta Venture's Most Respected Corporations (2007)
Recognized Intuit as Runner Up in the Most Respected Corporation category.

Hewitt Associates, Canada's 30 Best Benefit Plans
Intuit ranked ranked #1 in Alberta, #3 in Canada in 2007, ranked #2 in Alberta, #11 in Canada for 2008.

Alberta Premier's Award for Healthy Workplaces
Intuit received award in 2007.

Information about Intuit included in Road to Respect *was gathered from interviews Erica conducted with Jane Sillberg, former director of human resources, Intuit Canada. Any other sources used are identified with a footnote.*

KPMG

KPMG LLP is the Canadian member firm of KPMG, a global network of professional firms providing audit, tax, and advisory services. With over 123,000 people in 145 countries around the globe, KPMG is one of the largest professional services firms in the world. KPMG member firms respond to clients' complex business challenges across Canada and internationally.

Awards & Recognition

Canada's Top 100 Employers (2009)
Announced in *Maclean's* magazine.

Financial Post 10 Best Companies to Work For (2009)
Announced in the *National Post*.

Greater Toronto's Top 75 Employers (2009)
Announced in the *Toronto Star*.

The Top 40 Places Gen Y Wants to Work (2008)
Announced on Workopolis.

Best Employers for New Canadians (2008)
Announced in multiple major newspapers across Canada.

Canada's Best Diversity Employers (2008)
Announced in multiple major newspapers across Canada.

Best Workplace in Alberta for the Environmentally Conscious (2008)
Alberta Venture magazine.

National Capital Region "Employer of Distinction Award" (2007)
Ottawa Business Journal.

Fraser Valley Cultural Diversity Award
KPMG's Fraser Valley office was a winner at the Fraser Valley Cultural Diversity Awards in the "Reflective Workforce" category.

National Capital Region Employer of Distinction Award (2007)
The Ottawa office also received the National Capital Region Employer of Distinction Award for 2007. Organized by the Ottawa HR Forum, Talentmap and the *Ottawa Business Journal*, the Employer of Distinction Awards is a unique, employee-driven recognition program, offering workers a confidential opportunity to identify what makes their workplace exceptional.

Information about KPMG included in Road to Respect *was gathered from interviews Erica conducted with Val Duffey, HR director, communications & governance and from materials provided by Ms. Duffey and Beth Wilson, formerly chief human resources officer, currently national leader enterprise practice and Canadian managing partner. Any other sources used are identified with a footnote.*

SASKTEL

SaskTel is the leading full service communications provider in Saskatchewan, offering competitive voice, data, dial-up and high speed internet, entertainment and multimedia services, security, web hosting, text and messaging services, and cellular and wireless data services over its digital networks.

Awards & Recognition

A Top Employer

For the eighth consecutive year, SaskTel has been named one of Canada's Top 100 Employers. The list, compiled by Mediacorp Canada Inc., showcases companies with the country's best practices in managing what many businesses call their greatest asset – their people. SaskTel is the only Saskatchewan-based company to achieve this distinction eight years in a row.

Live & Learn: SaskTel achieves ASTD award

In recognition of a corporate commitment to employee training, SaskTel has been recognized with an American Society for Training and Development (ASTD) BEST Award for 2007. ASTD is the leading association for workplace learning and performance professionals. With more than 40,000 members, ASTD advocates for continuous learning and performance improvement to drive the global economy. The ASTD BEST Awards recognize organizations that demonstrate enterprise-wide success or achievement as a result of employee learning.

Best Workplaces in Canada

SaskTel was selected as one of the Best Workplaces in Canada by the Great Places To Work Institute. SaskTel was featured in the April 10, 2006 *Canadian Business* magazine article.

AGEN Industry Award for Aboriginal Participation

SaskTel received the 2006 AGEN (Aboriginal Government Employees Network) Industry Award for Aboriginal Participation. It is the latest recognition for the company's commitment to strengthening its relationships with aboriginal communities by promoting business development, career opportunities and overall corporate commitment.

Interprovincial Association for Native Employment (IANE) Ivan Ahenakew Award

SaskTel won the Interprovincial Association for Native Employment (IANE) Ivan Ahenakew Award for outstanding contributions to the employment of aboriginal peoples. This award is given to any business, company, government department or aboriginal organization that has shown results in the areas of Recruitment and Training of Aboriginal personnel for employment and training for the current year.

Information about SaskTel included in Road to Respect *was gathered from interviews Erica conducted with Carolynne Warner, manager of human resources. Any other sources used are identified with a footnote.*

Canada Safeway

Canada Safeway is a leading retail supermarket chain in western Canada. It has about 214 stores and about twenty-five percent of the grocery market in western Canada. Parent company Safeway is one of the leading supermarket operators in the U.S. Canada Safeway serves independent grocery stores and institutional customers through four distribution centres; it also has about a dozen Canadian plants that make or process meat, dairy products, fruits and vegetables, bread, and other foods.

At Safeway, the diversity of our employees, customers, and the communities in which we operate is a key ingredient in our success.

- We value and celebrate the diversity of the men and women who make up our workforce;
- We respect the personal worth and unique contributions of each individual; and
- We expect that each of us grant others the same respect, cooperation and fair treatment that we seek for ourselves.

—Excerpt from Safeway's Corporate Diversity Policy

Awards & Recognition

Corporate Employer of the Year (2008)
DIVERSEcity Community Resources Society.

Employer Recognition Award (2008)
MOSAIC (Multilingual Orientation Service Association for Immigrant Communities).

Employer Recognition Award (2008)
Minister's Council on Employment for Persons with Disabilities, Government of BC.

Employer of the Year (2008)
Greater Vancouver Business Leadership Network (a Program of BC Centre for Ability).

Business of the Year (2007)
Manitoba Business Leadership Network.

Employer of the Year (2007)
Canadian Down Syndrome Society.

Diversity Award (2007)
Edmonton Chamber of Commerce.

Award of Merit (2007)
BC Centre for Abilities.

Corporate Employer of the Year (2007)
DIVERSEcity Resources Society.

Bridging the Gap Award (2006)
Saskatchewan Youth Employment Centre.

Recognition Award (2006)
THEO BC (BC Society of Training for Health and Employment Opportunities).

Employer of the Year (2006)
Canadian Immigrant magazine.

Business of the Year (2005)
Manitoba Business Leadership Network.

Top 50 Employers for Minorities (2005)
Fortune magazine.

2003 Celebration of Excellence Award
Disability Resource Network of BC.

Information about Canada Safeway included in Road to Respect *was gathered from interviews Erica conducted with Cliff Yeo, advisor, human resources department and Scott Gibney, public affairs manager. Any other sources used are identified with a footnote.*